ADVANCED PRAISE FOR

A JOURNEY WITH CHILDREN AND CHARACTERS

The book A Journey with Children and Characters is profoundly enlightening with stories of heartbreakers and heroes. It truly is a journey with spurious and interesting characters, vulnerable children, and many revelations.
  -Trenton W. Valparisious, 30-year public school teacher

McGiboney takes us along on his journey and talks to us as if we are all riding on the same school bus. Interspersed with moments in history and professional theory, the light shines a little brighter on the stories. The book begs to be read.
    -McGuire Van Groton, School Psychologist

A fascinating book with many characters, and it includes children looking to adults for care and comfort. It's a good book but some stories are haunting.
      -W. Anne Claxton Peguire, Parent

Few books hold my attention like this one did. It's not a literary work; it's not an autobiography; it's not a book about education; instead, it's a very human book. A book about what matters.
      -Juan Sherringston-Phillipe, Bilingual Therapist

A Child's Love

It comes into our view, but we don't see it in the rush of the day.

It's there for us to notice and cherish every day.

It doesn't ask for anything in return but it's there every day.

Sunday to Sunday, morning to night, a child's love is waiting for us every day.

Timberline of the Mind

A Journey with Children and Characters

Garry W. McGiboney, Ph.D.

CAMBRIDGE CHANNEL PRESS

A Journey with Children and Characters

Published by Cambridge Channel Press an imprint of Leighbrough Printing, LLC
673421ki2345

Library of Congress Cataloging-in-Publication Data
British Library Cataloging-Publication Data
Print ISBN – 9780-9979629-7-0
Library ISBN – 0680322016
(Excerpts from *The Private Side of Public Education* by Garry McGiboney are used with permission from the publisher.)

A Journey with Children and Characters
    1. Psychology – Educational
    2. School Psychology – Developmental Studies
    3. Academic – Motivational Studies

Printed and distributed in the United States by Reveltree Distribution

DEDICATION

This book is dedicated to educators who understand the value and necessity of creating a positive school climate for all children for all the right reasons at all times.

Other Books by Garry W. McGiboney

The Psychology of School Climate

Crisis Management Planning

The Psychology of Leadership Practices, Principles, and Priorities

Daily Wisdom and Inspiration

Leading Us Out of Darkness

Timberline of the Mind

TABLE OF CONTENTS

PROLOGUE

The educator/philosopher, John Dewey, said, "Education is a social process; education is growth; education is not preparation for life but is life itself."

This book is a story about children. It is also a book about heroes, anti-heroes, wannabes, saviors, demons, and angels-a full cast of characters. It was said by Shakespeare that with a well-rounded cast of characters, the story will take care of itself because dynamic energy is created between characters as a natural occurrence of human interaction. The interactions between children and characters are fueled by contrasts, conflicting interests, sacrifice, intrigue, needs, trauma, self-absorption, and human drama.

Put a cast of characters in a story, add children, and the plot will evolve. A plot that surrounds a story that spans decades and includes characters determined to control others and circumstances or who would sacrifice their soul to help children. Then there are other characters whose naiveté is noble but ignorant, well-intended but short-sighted.

This book follows a journey with children and characters from many different perspectives and experiences. Some stories are inspiring, some are troubling, some are complex, but all are real.

PART ONE

OUR CHILDREN'S JOURNEYS

Until the age of eight, the boy was typical. He enjoyed his friends, loved to watch baseball, and was a good student at school. He had two older brothers that shared some of the same friends and enjoyment of baseball. At the end of the summer, just after he celebrated his 8th birthday, something changed. He claimed he saw things on the walls at home. For example, he asked his brothers one day who stuck the baseball on the wall in his bedroom. When his brothers looked at the wall, they saw nothing. The boy thought they were kidding him. At dinner one night, he asked his mother to pass him the French fries. She laughed and said, "I guess you wish we had some." He seemed puzzled by her reply and asked again if he could have the French fries. They were not there. In the restroom at school one day, the boy couldn't understand why the toilets were so tall and the sink was almost on the floor.

I was the school psychologist that evaluated the boy and observed him in school. It seemed that the boy's depth perception was off and he was hallucinating. I observed him trying to wipe something off the wall repeatedly, but nothing was there. The evaluation results were unusual as was the behavior I observed. It seemed that the problem was neurological instead of psychopathic, so I consulted with a psychiatrist at a nearby medical college. After spending a lot of time with the boy and after consulting with other psychiatrists, the boy was diagnosed with a very rare mental condition called Todd Syndrome, which is a neurologic condition in which a patient's sense of body image and space are distorted and includes hallucinations and sensory and spatial distortions. Further examinations revealed a brain tumor. The student had surgery to remove the tumor but for several months thereafter, he still experienced imagery distortions and other neurological issues that required extensive physical, occupational, and speech therapy. Two years later, the student was well-adjusted and active in school and other activities.

The 15-year-old student was sent to an alternative school because of chronic fighting. He was a short, muscular boy with a permanent scowl on his face. The other students at the alternative school avoided him. They sensed his anger and knew he wasn't afraid of anyone. The student quietly settled into the routine of the school and caused no problems. He avoided the other students and they were content to leave him alone. Overtime, the teachers realized that the student was brilliant even though his transcript showed poor grades in all subject areas. The teachers spent time with him and encouraged him. He returned their positive attitude with extra effort and excellent work. He had all A's in his classes and was seen occasionally with a smile. Teachers and counselors told the student that he had college potential. The student told one teacher that he had never heard a positive word from his parents or his teachers.

One day the student was walking down the hall while changing classes when one of his favorite teachers walked to catch up with and put his hand of the student's back near his neck as a symbol of support, but the student in a brief moment of fury turned quickly and punched the teacher in the face knocking him to the floor. The student was stunned when he realized what he had done. He looked around as if to run; instead, he bent down over the teacher and with tears streaming down his face apologized. This was a violent act that could lead to expulsion and incarceration. The teacher, counselor, school resource officer, and I met with the student to understand what happened. The student's father choked him on a regular basis and abused him in other ways. His father's method of choking him was to sneak up behind him and grab his neck and choke him until the student passed out. When the teacher put his hand on that same spot of his back and neck, the student's reaction was taking a swing at his father not at his teacher. The teacher refused to press charges and we met in the Juvenile Court judge's chambers to discuss the situation. The judge said the student cannot get away with that without consequences. So he was allowed to return to school after 10 days and his probation was extended until the end of the school year. The student continued his good work and left the alternative school with more credits in one year than he earned in three previous year. He completed his time at the alternative school with excellent grades. He then attended a non-traditional high school where he graduated. In my mailbox one day several years later, I found an invitation to his college graduation.

The third-grade girl was referred to me for a psychological evaluation because she did not interact with the other students, often stared off into space, and she did not respond when teachers tried to get her attention. Most days on the playground she would go off by herself and appear to be talking to an imaginary person. The girl, however, was very smart, always completed her homework, and made high marks on all her school work.

She did not want to talk to me during the psychological evaluation, but she found the tasks challenging and she attacked them with enthusiasm and skill. She completed all timed task ahead of time and she excelled on all achievement tests. She was willing to talk in short sentences about school and her interest in reading, math, and artwork. She refused to talk to me about her home, siblings, parents, classmates, or teacher. During the parent conference, the girl's mother was very nervous and almost seemed afraid. A soft inquiry finally revealed that the little girl had no siblings and no friends in the apartment complex which was occupied primarily by elderly citizens. The mother broke down crying when she revealed that the little girl spends all her time at home alone and had lived like that for at least four years. The mother had to work two jobs for several hour each day and night. She was not at home in the morning and did not arrive home until after 8:00 in the evening. The mother's income was not enough to hire a baby sitter. The little girl fixed her dinner; bathed herself; did her homework; put herself to bed; woke herself up in the morning; prepared her breakfast; clothed herself; and made it to the school bus stop. They had no television and the small radio only picked-up a couple of radio stations. The little girl did most of the laundry and other housework. Loneliness was her constant companion and it was hindering her social growth. The mother was connected with a local church and United Way. The little girl caught a van to an after-school program and the church took her home each afternoon around 6:30. United Way arranged for the children in the afterschool program to take a box dinner home. It took time, but gradually the little girl developed friends and her social isolation ended. She became more participatory at school and her expressive language skills improved.

From the day he was born until the day he got into serious trouble at age 15, he lived in a home that filled his day with trauma. His father and then later his mother's boyfriends constantly told the boy that he was a "sorry" human being. Daily and under all types of circumstances, the boy was told that he was "sorry" – worthless. The boy was quiet and never talked back even though the anger grew inside every year and every time he heard that he was a "sorry" person. He knew in his heart he was not worthless – a "sorry" human being, but he heard it every day as part of his trauma-laced home life. The boy's salvation was school. He was quiet but he had a few friends and he enjoyed the school work, the orderliness, and cleanliness of the school. He seldom had enough food at home, so he savored school breakfast and lunch. Some teachers encouraged him, but he didn't feel like he could talk to any of his teachers or counselor about his home. He didn't want to get his mother into trouble. One day after being yelled at all morning and even as he left his house, he heard the live-in boyfriend yell "you're just plain sorry – worthless."

The school bully pushed him at school that day and without thinking he turned around and hit the bully so forcefully it knocked him unconscious and he stopped breathing. The bully was revived and rushed to the hospital. The 15-year-old boy was sent to juvenile court. The judge could not get much of a response from the student, so he said, "Tell me this – are you sorry?" The 15-year-old blurted out loud, "No I'm not sorry." The judge grew angry and said since the boy showed no remorse, he would spend time in jail to think about what he did. A court social worker who had been trained on language deficits finally put the pieces together and reported to me and the judge that the word "sorry" had a different meaning to the boy. The judge ordered a language and psychological evaluation. The clinician found that the student suffered from Post-Traumatic Stress Disorder and had language skill deficits in expressive and receptive language. The judge's order shifted from detention to speech and language therapy.

The quiet 13-year-old boy was socially awkward and only had a small circle of friends when he entered middle school. He was, however, an excellent student who excelled in math and science. His goal was to attend Georgia Tech. His parents were well educated and held good career jobs. The family included two other children that were older and successful in college. The family had typical issues but otherwise was healthy and happy. The 13-year-old boy wanted to be more popular and have more friends, but he wasn't sure how to do that. He observed others and he tried to model their behavior, but it didn't work for him. One day, a very popular and pretty girl joined by a couple of her friends approached the boy and said they made a list of girls that were interested in talking with him but he had to sign the paper so the girls would know he was serious. He eagerly signed the paper. The next day when he arrived at school the school was in turmoil. Some of the girls were crying and some of the boys bumped the boy around for no apparent reason. As one of his friends said, "I can't believe you did that," the school principal called his name and took him to the office. He held up the paper and said, "Why did you put this list together? How were you planning to attack them?" The boy was terrified when he saw the list with his signature at the bottom of the paper. It was the list of girls he saw the previous day but above the fold line was this statement, "This is my list of girls I'm going to shoot." The boy was completed puzzled and he told the principal and his parents that he signed a paper, but it didn't have the threat on it. The student was suspended out of school and was facing expulsion at a tribunal hearing. He was devastated as was his family. The parents asked for an investigation by the school district, which was assigned to me. When I met with the boy, it was obvious that the student did not have the maturity of forethought to devise such a scheme. He cried almost the entire time he told his side of the story. I contacted the parents of the girls and met them with their daughters at the school. The first thing I asked the parents was, "Do you recognize any handwriting on this letter?" The father of one of the girls confronted his daughter because he recognized her writing. The other parents also recognized their daughter's writing. The truth spilled out. The principal did not take the time to investigate because he had several parents demanding "justice." The student was put back in school. The rescued student sent me a note saying that when he wins the Nobel Prize in Physics he would call my name during his acceptance speech. He did not win the Nobel Prize in Physics; instead, he studied architecture and graduated with honors from Georgia Tech.

The smart, always happy and gregarious 5th grader came to school on a Monday with the same clothes she wore the previous Friday. Her hair was unkempt, and her smile was gone. She did not speak to anyone even when her friends asked her what was wrong. The teacher who took time to know her students noticed something wasn't right with the girl as soon as she walked into the classroom. She did not want to draw too much attention to the girl in class, so she waited until the lunch break to take the girl to the counseling office. The girl did not want to talk. When the teacher said she had to go back to class, the girl burst out crying and said, "Don't leave." The teacher asked the secretary to cover her class for the next few minutes and the teacher told the girl that she'd be right back. When the teacher came back into the counselor's office, the girl jumped up and hugged the teacher while crying. We learned that the girl's mother walked out on the family leaving three young children with the father who was ill prepared to take care of three girls. They found some fresh clothes for the girl; the teacher washed her face and brushed her hair and tied her hair with a bow. The girl hugged the teacher again and said she was ready to go back to class. The teacher and girl walked hand-in-hand to class. I was brought in on the case and I contacted the girl's father to tell him what happened. He was grateful and asked for help. The counselor referred him to a local program called Kind with Care that helps single parents. The 5th grade teacher was the girl's idol and role model. She adored the teacher and was ashamed of her appearance that day because her father did not know how to care for her. When the girl saw her teacher leaving the counseling office it was like watching her mother leave the home. That's why she cried out for the teacher. The teacher could have said, "I must get back to my class." Instead, she went back to the girl. Kind with Care went to the home and worked with the father on child care essentials and provided clothes and personal items for all of the girls. The Kind with Care staff took the father and his daughters to the local Goodwill store to show them how to shop and provided them with a list of groceries and other items they would need. Kind with Care connected the father with a local church that provided abandonment support. The little girl's smile returned and she thrived in school.

The teacher returned to her classroom the day after she attended professional learning day on mental health awareness. Her 8th grade classes were filled with students from a wide variety of backgrounds, experiences, and abilities. Some were very intelligent, some struggled academically, some were artistic, and some were gregarious while others were shy. She had a few students that were behavior problems. She had tried talking to them, acknowledging good behavior and other methods but she often sent them to the disciplinary office for disruptive and disrespectful behavior. There was one student who seemed to fluctuate between attentive and disruptive. The teacher could not predict which she would see on any given day from the girl. At the workshop on mental health, the teacher learned what mental health was and what may be signs of mental health distress. She relived that training on a day when the student was being disrespectful to everyone in the class. Instead of sending the student out of class to the assistant principal of discipline she decided that day to send her to the counselor. The counselor did not know the student, so he spent time learning about her. The counselor called me in to also talk to the girl. I observed her closely and I noticed a slight droop on the left side of the student's mouth and while talking sometimes the student's face seemed to stiffen. During the conversation, the student's mood changed, and she slowly became agitated for no apparent reason. The counselor called the student's mother who said the girl was pleasant most of the time, but her moodiness and agitation seemed to be more frequent. Nothing had changed at home and the girl seemed to be in good health after she had a non-descript virus several months previously. I suggested to the mother that her daughter should have a full physical exam. The doctors diagnosed Bell's palsy which can develop after a virus. The student was self-conscious about her appearance, she knew her face was distorted slightly, even though no one seemed to notice the problem. She received counseling for the problem and physical therapy as she learned to cope with the palsy. Her moodiness leveled out. Her teacher asked if she wanted to tell the class about Bell's palsy and to the teacher's surprise the student said yes. When the other students heard her story, they comforted her and supported her.

Restorative practice is a method to hold a person accountable to his or her victim by talking with them in a controlled setting. Sometimes the practice is used in school settings and more often assigned in juvenile court. The facilitator shares a report on the restorative practice session with the juvenile judge. Roy, a 15-year-old was assigned restorative practice with his bullying victim under strict supervision. During the session, the only comments Roy made were "dunno," "yea," "I guess so" – just short replies. The facilitator became annoyed at Roy and dismissed the session. The facilitator told an observer of the session that Roy will be in trouble with the judge because of his lack of interest and participation in the restorative practice session. The observer, who had training in speech and language pathology poised the question: "Do you think Roy has the language skills necessary to participate in restorative practice?" The facilitator said, "We've never thought about that." Roy was given a language assessment and it was found that he had a language disorder that interferes with both his receptive and expressive language abilities. He received speech and language therapy. The student's attention span improved, his articulation improved, and he became a much better student while developing positive social skills. His case in juvenile court was handled much differently than the original adjudication order. Instead of placement in a detention center, the student was put on probation that was contingent upon him attending language sessions regularly and on time.

Everyone said the 12-year-old boy was a problem since the first grade. He was restless, disrespectful, rude, and often disrupted classes. The other students stayed away from him because he was always getting into trouble. His behavior at home was similar. Many parent-teacher conferences turned into comforting sessions – where the teachers consoled the parents and the parents consoled the teachers. A referral to a clinical psychologist led to the recommendation that the student be referred to a state psychiatric residential treatment center (RTF) to stabilize his behavior. All new arrivals at the RTF undergo a rigorous series of tests, including mental health, hearing, vision, speech and language, nutritional health, oral health, and cardiovascular health screenings. The results of the routine evaluation revealed many surprises. The student failed the vision test, hearing test, nutrition test, and had gum disease. These issues are usually found in low-income homes and are not typical in middle class homes. The student was fitted for glasses; he received a hearing aid; and he was put on a nutritional diet plan to help him gain some of the weight and strength he had lost, and he received regular treatments from an orthodontist. His behavior changed immediately. He went to bed before 10:00 pm and slept soundly instead of pacing up and down the hallways at night like he had done for years. His behavior at school changed markedly. He still had issues like other students but he worked through them and listened to adults. He learned to socialize and self-regulate. Although it was difficult to change the attitudes of teachers, students, and others about the student because they had him pegged as a "trouble maker," over time that changed, and the student became more successful and clearly happy.

She was reading chapter books at age 3, winning chess matches with adults at age 9, and studying Calculus at age 11. She was inpatient, forceful, stubborn, and she knew she was the smartest student in the classroom. She thought she knew more than most teachers and found other students her age immature and boring. She never played with dolls or other toys. She was cut off from the social world because she did not like people. Her parents were baffled by their daughter. They had typical social lives with visiting friends and neighbors, and they participated in social activities including school and community activities. They encouraged their daughter to join social activities, but she refused. The girl made all of the decisions about her life; her parents never pushed anything she didn't want to do. Her older brother was gregarious and popular at school. He ignored his sister and referred to her as "weird." The common opinion was to "leave her alone."

I told the parents with the support of the school counselor that allowing the girl to make all of the decisions would be the path of least resistance but in the long run would be unhealthy and unfair for the girl. She had to learn how to interact with people. She was added to a small counseling group at school although she resisted and refused to talk during the first few sessions. The parents, with encouragement, made their daughter join a chess club at the local public library. She refused to get out of the car at the first meeting but eventually capitulated. Within six months, the girl was a vocal participant in the counseling sessions but she had to learn how to interact with the others which had bad, awkward moments and good moments. She was learning about the social world through trial and error. The chess club allowed her to learn social skills while challenging her intellect. She enjoyed the chess club and never missed a session. She became more social and interactive. As her parents became more assertive about social activities, the girl became more willing to participate. The tough love at school and at home turned the little girl's life around.

The 10-year-old boy had been in ten foster families in less than five years. It was not because he was difficult to deal with in the first few foster homes, but he became temperamental without warning. He went from casually friendly to obstinate and resistant. The moves were not always because of him; some foster families moved and at least two decided they could no longer handle the financial pressures of being a foster parent. Eventually, the boy resented the moves and lack of stability. The boy was viewed as moody at the schools he attended. It was difficult to determine or measure his academic progress or skills because he moved so often – seven schools in five years. He was referred to me for an evaluation because his school performance was declining, and his moodiness was growing worse, and he was exhibiting some aggressive behavior. The school nurse reported to me that the student frequently asked to see the school nurse where he asked for Tylenol. When asked what was hurting, he would just say "never mind; it's okay." My evaluation revealed an above average intellect with slightly below grade level reading and math skills. He was certainly capable of doing the school work. I talked to the school nurse who reported that after the student's third visit to the school nurse, she decided that something was wrong. I asked the nurse if she noticed that he seemed to limp slightly and when he sit down his posture was not straight. She agreed. The nurse contacted the boy's foster care case supervisor and recommended that he have a physical exam immediately. It was quickly arranged. The examining doctor suspected an orthopedic problem and referred him to a specialist. It was confirmed that the boy was suffering from painful juvenile rheumatoid arthritis (JRS). A treatment plan was developed; the case worker was informed, and she shared the diagnosis and treatment plan with the school. The doctor explained JRA to the boy and how it would be treated. The doctor said they could manage the pain that he had quietly suffered with for years. Pain-free, the boy was a different child. He was friendly, enjoyed school work, participated in sports, and joined the Boy Scouts where he loved to earn badges. He even earned a badge on JRA.

She had difficulty making and keeping friends because she wanted close, personal, and intense relationships, which drove others away. Seemingly, everything in her life was intense. Her parents were constantly telling her to calm down. Her reactions ranged from overly excited joy or deep intense depression episodes. She could not seem to regulate herself and she frequently complained about stomach pain. A clinical psychologist diagnosed her as Borderline Personality Disorder and started Dialectal Therapy in individual and group sessions. The girl's ongoing upset stomach was attributed to her high levels of anxiety. Her anxiety level grew worse and she began to lose weight. She told her mother that something was wrong because her stomach hurt all of the time and she always felt like something was about to happen to her. She developed insomnia and said she didn't feel well enough to be around her friends. She was referred to me because of concerns about her behavior and academic performance. During the evaluation, the girl said she constantly worried about her health. She talked more about her physical condition and ailments than her psychological issues. I recommended that the parents take her to a gastroenterologist. She was diagnosed with Celiac disease, an inherited autoimmune digestive disorder in which affected individuals cannot tolerate gluten and several other products. Irritability and depression are common symptoms in children with this disorder. The doctor started her on an aggressive treatment to increase fiber, iron, calcium, magnesium, zinc, folate, niacin, riboflavin, vitamin B_{12}, and vitamin D, as well as copper and vitamin B_6. Within two weeks she was feeling better and her anxiety had diminished significantly.

Her parents watched her reach developmental milestones several months and then years later than expected. The pediatrician said the little girl's development should be watched carefully to determine if she might need "special support services" at some time in the future. They sought resources and experts in developmental issues and exposed her to various interventions to stimulate her development. They noticed little things that seemed to contradict her apparent developmental delays; for example, she excitedly pointed at a 25-piece puzzle with a picture of a kitten on the box. They bought her the puzzle because she seemed to love the picture. The mother went into her daughter's bedroom a few days later and saw the puzzle completed on the little table by the girl's bed. She asked her husband when he put the puzzle together and he said he did not put it together. They bought a similar puzzle with a picture of a puppy. They sat with their daughter and watched her methodically put the puzzle together. The pediatrician did not think it was possible. As the little girl grew older, it was apparent that her behavior was not typical and there were flashes of high intelligence. I encouraged the parents to have their daughter evaluated on the Marcus Autism Center. The Center discovered that the little girl had a high level of intelligence, was very creative, had a special talent for organization and logistics, and was autistic. She entered the autism program and within one year made substantial progress with the help of the center, her parents, the child care center, and the public kindergarten staff. She is in a typical kindergarten class and is functioning very well. She has a circle of friends that support her, also. Her friends enjoy watching her put puzzles together.

PART TWO

A JOURNEY WITH LIFE

CHAPTER 1
A SIMPLE LIFE

We spend the first twelve months of our children's lives
teaching them to walk and talk and the next twelve years
telling them to sit down and shut up.
—Phyllis Diller

I lived in a rural part of a county that was very quickly transforming into a suburban area. My parents were uneducated but very hardworking and salt-of-the-earth people tempered, shaped, and tested by the Great Depression and World War II. My father was a self-taught mechanic and my mother worked most of her adult life on an assembly line at a paper company. They loved their family; they loved their community; they loved the community church, and they loved their country. They appreciated a good day's work, friends, a simple meal, good health, and public education. They put their entire faith in teachers and administrators to do the right thing without question.

When I first attended public school, I took my parents' faith with me – teachers were golden, and the Golden Rule was Gospel.

My first-grade year in public school was filled with wonderful discoveries and new experiences. Our little country school had about 200 students in grades one through seven. Our first-grade teacher could make Dick and Jane jump off the pages and pull up a chair and talk about their simple but meaningful lives with us. We were motivated by stories of famous people and their seemingly impossible feats. A trip to the school's library was like a trip around the world. The teacher brought life to the classroom, the library, the playground, on field trips, and even in the tiny school cafeteria. The teacher worked with students who were struggling and challenged those students who were clearly ahead of the rest of us. That is now called "differentiated instruction" when in fact it is just good teaching. The teacher made every effort to ensure that the classroom climate was positive, which many times included tending to the unique needs of the children. There were many days when children needed every ounce of compassion the teacher could offer.

One day a very shy little girl had an accident at her desk. She was too quiet and embarrassed to tell anyone but shortly an odor gave away the nature of her accident. She started to quietly cry. The teacher quickly went to the little girl's desk and kneeled beside her. She talked quietly to her for a few moments and then the teacher stood up and announced to the class that she would like for each student to take out a pencil and a piece of paper and draw a picture of our favorite animal.

As the rest of us were busy looking for paper and pencil she quietly escorted the little girl out of the class. A short time later, the teacher and the little girl returned to class. As soon as the teacher walked into the classroom, she asked who wanted to share their picture. That way no one was staring at the little girl as she quickly and quietly returned to her desk. I don't know how the teacher did it, but the little girl was wearing a different dress and she had a sparkling smile on her face. The teacher loved and protected the students and we loved her.

Toward the end of the school year, our teacher was out of school for about a week. The principal introduced our substitute teacher and informed us that our teacher's father had passed away.

The first day our teacher returned to school she looked so sad. She tried gamely to put on a happy face, and she tended to us as always, but it was obvious even to us that she was sad. At one point in the day, as we were completing work at our desk, the teacher could not hold back her tears any longer. She sat at her desk crying. The entire classroom of 19 students, little girls and boys not more than six years old, got out of our desks at the same time and spontaneously stood in front of her desk. A little girl asked the teacher if she was okay. The teacher walked from around her desk, kneeled on the floor and opened her arms to all us. Imagine the scene of 19 little girls and boys giving our beloved teacher a group hug. We were all crying and hugging at the same time. The memory of that special moment still brings tears to my eyes.

Second grade was wholesomely wonderful, too. I was into reading and learning–everything was fun and rewarding. I would chatter almost non-stop at our family dinner table about school. I liked the routine of each school day, the reassurance of a safe, secure, and nurturing school climate. I found enormous comfort knowing that my teacher cared about me and all of us. I even enjoyed the school bus ride with our bespectacled whistling bus driver who always had a band-aid to support one side of his sagging glasses. Whatever reason he had for wearing the band-aid, it certainly didn't slow down his bus or aggravate his good nature. He was a man determined that school buses are a safe haven for children. He also firmly believed that school buses should arrive and depart on time, even if kids were slung from one side of the bus to the other and back, and we enjoyed every minute of it. We did not mind the dust rolling through the bus windows on those hot late spring or early autumn days, as our beloved bus driver barreled down dirt roads. But he was more than a bus driver; he was our friend and guardian. He knew our parents and he knew us. He noticed when something was wrong; when a student was upset. He knew the value of a smile and how a word of encouragement could lift a child's spirit. He did not tolerate misbehavior, but he could laugh at the rambunctious enthusiasm and the silliness of childhood. He even showed interest in our show and tell projects, including my pickled tonsils.

I had my tonsils removed when I was in the second grade. As was traditional in those days, the hospital preserved the tonsils in a jar and give to the child. I brought my tonsils to the bus and then to school in a jar. The bus driver laughed out loud when I proudly handed him the jar. The teacher turned this gross item into a teachable moment about the human body even as she held the jar as far away from her body as possible.

During that same school year, I swallowed a nickel and had to have it removed at a children's hospital. The teacher and the bus driver both called our home to check on me and when I returned to school the teacher transformed my return into a welcome but also into a lesson about personal safety. She was an amazing and perceptive teacher with a good heart for children and who knew the importance of a positive classroom climate.

Near Christmas, a new student arrived in our second-grade class. The teacher introduced the little boy in a way that did not embarrass him. When we went to lunch that day, the little boy stopped outside the cafeteria door. The teacher went to him to see what was wrong. I'm not certain why he stopped and refused to enter the cafeteria, but I think it was because he had no money because I saw the teacher give him a quarter, the cost of our lunch. Several times that year, I saw the teacher slip a quarter into the hands of students on the way to the cafeteria. She had a way of checking on all of us that was nurturing and not embarrassing. She would come up behind us and place her hand on our shoulders and encourage us to eat our lunch. Her reassuring touch meant the world to us. I'm certain there were some children whose only contact with another person was that gentle touch from our second-grade teacher.

That was the same school year I took the "double-dog dare" that I could not swallow a prune seed without choking. I did swallow it, but I did choke. Students gathered around to watch my skin color change from Irish white to blueberry blue. Teachers rushed over immediately and repeatedly slapped my back. Then the burly PE teacher grabbed me from behind and squeezed the prune out. For a fleeting moment, I was a hero because our weekly serving of prunes was replaced with the return of our much-appreciated small square sugar cakes. The school thought replacing delicious, sugar-packed little cakes with healthy prunes would go unnoticed by the students. I stopped progressive thoughts about healthy desserts in its tracks.

The drama of my prune episode took place while our teacher sat with other teachers at the grown-up's table. Upon witnessing the prune event, she decided it would be best if she sat quietly with her class during lunch for the rest of the school year. She didn't seem to mind. It was apparent in many ways that she enjoyed teaching and loved her students.

All the joy, my wonderful attitude toward school, the positive classroom climate, the belief that teachers were heaven-sent stopped suddenly in the third grade and public education for me was never quite the same.

At times during my life well into my adulthood, I have thought about how much my experience with public education changed in one year, and how that experience shaped so much of my life thereafter personally and professionally. Talk to anyone about their school experience and you will see them drift off into a corner of their memory palace to a place of joy or sorrow or both. School climate and classroom climate stays with us for a lifetime, positive or negative, and that climate is determined by the teacher not the students.

CHAPTER 2
DARK CORNERS

*A poor surgeon hurts one person at a time. A poor
teacher hurts 130.*
–Ernest Boyer

The dark corner of my memory palace is still inhabited by
my third-grade teacher and the negative classroom climate
she created. She was everything opposite from my first and
second-grade teachers, who had shown me how wonderful
a teacher could and should be and how a positive classroom
climate can be an emotional safe haven and a protective
factor for children.

The third-grade teacher's day was not complete
unless she terrified students with her loud verbal blasts and
her spider-like movement around the classroom. If she saw
something nondescript that she didn't like, she would bolt
out from around her desk and grab the offending student
by the ear or grab a student's hand, turn it over and paddle
the open palm with a ruler at such a furious pace and with
so much anger it was terrifying. If I student cried out,
"*What did I do?*" sometimes she would say, "*Nothing – just
your turn.*" She was cruel and she enjoyed her cruelty and
intimidation.

We could not understand why there were birthdays
in the first and second grade and even in the other third-
grade classroom but none in my third-grade classroom.
How and why would this teacher ignore our birthdays? Just
as troubling, there was no recognition of holidays. During
Halloween week we could hear other classrooms having a
grand time with their sounds of laughter and merriment

drifting down the hallway. And why were we ignoring other holidays? No crayon hand-turkeys for Thanksgiving. No Christmas decorations or Christmas-tree shaped cookies with glitter. No Christmas Party. It was a cold and heartless classroom.

The teacher did not believe in field trips and not once during the third grade did we visit the school library. Where plants and artwork brightened other classrooms, my third grade classroom was absent anything other than a teacher's desk, student desks, a chalkboard that was never cleaned or used for any purpose, a worn rack for student's coats, and a stack of newspapers in the back corner of the room that some of us believed contained the remains of previous students stuffed like so many butterflies between the pages. The classroom was an atmosphere of doom and anxiety every day. The window shades were always closed to purposefully block any effort to let sunshine into the classroom and the teacher covered the hallway door window with a sheet of black paper.

That year I cried on the way to school most days and I refused to tell anyone why. I didn't even tell our bus driver who often asked what was wrong. Many students in that classroom cried, and no one took the time to find out why. We picked at our lunches and stood listlessly outside during physical education. I internalized the anxiety and terror as did many of the other students.

The smell of sweet perfume, flowers, crayons and that intoxicating aroma of a freshly cleaned chalkboard in other classrooms were replaced with a musty, dusty, chemical-like smell in my third-grade classroom. Some students whimpered all day, and some clinched their desks so tightly they had blisters on each finger before the end of

September. Some students wet their clothes during class and sat in it for most of the day, totally from fear of the teacher. But that wasn't the worst of it.

One student was very large for his age, awkward and unusually clumsy. He wore the same shirt and pants almost every day; obviously, he was from a poor family. He had a slight speech impediment and he was very self-conscious and shy. The first and second-grade teachers worked with him and even brought him clothes. The cafeteria staff brought small bags of food for him to take home to his family. He survived and thrived on the kindness of the teachers and the positive climate of the classroom and the support of other adults in the school. He was nurtured in the first and second grade.

I still cringe when I recall the degree of cruelty that poor kid suffered at the hands of the third-grade teacher. She intentionally embarrassed him almost every day, and she encouraged other students to shun him. One student was very cruel to him and bullied and harassed him daily with encouragement from the teacher. *"Go take a sniff of Stinky,"* the teacher would say, and sure enough some students would make sniffing noises. By the midpoint of the school year, a few students were modeling the cruelty of the teacher and how she treated students.

I rode on the same bus with the harassed student and I saw the house he came out of each morning and went back to each afternoon. The house stood lopsided from age and neglect with trash in the yard, tattered clothes hanging from a makeshift clothesline, and a constant stream of smoke from a small fire near the corner of the house with an indescribable odor. This gentle, quiet, shy boy only had school to escape from his deplorable home situation. The first and second-grade teachers did what they could to make the boy's life meaningful. Yet in the third grade, all he got every day was a mean-spirited teacher and a classroom that was crueler than his living conditions at home.

One day on the school playground, the teacher continued making fun of the student's size and clumsiness in front of other students. We were bouncing a basketball and passing it to each other. He could not dribble a basketball and he could not catch a basketball, but he was forced to endure the humiliation. The teacher laughed and made snide comments about the student. There stood this gentle giant of a student with tears rolling down his face from embarrassment and humiliation and she enjoyed it. The teacher's pet went up to the sobbing boy and started making fun of him for crying. What happened next was burned in my mind for a lifetime, as it was for all who witnessed it. The gentle giant grabbed his harasser by the throat and lifted him off the ground. He was choking him to death, literally. The teacher started screaming and other teachers on the playground ran over to see what was wrong. At least four teachers frantically tried to talk him into letting the student loose while pulling at his arms and hands. Everyone that day learned how strong he was, especially for his age. With tears still running down his face and with the flailing student still in the death grip, he looked around at everybody as if seeing them for the first time. He let go of the student and started running. The teacher's toad survived, much to the disappointment of many of us, and we all went back to the third-grade dungeon classroom. We could not wait to see our gentle giant classmate on the bus that afternoon to tell him how much we all appreciated his efforts to destroy the class bully, but he was not there, and he was not on the bus the next day or any day after that. We never saw him again.

For a lifetime, I have wondered what happened to him, but in my heart, I know what happened. His family was told that he could not come to school anymore. It was done that way in those days. I must take my memory somewhere else to cope – for to think of that gentle boy sitting in that rundown, depressing, and soul-destroying house all day and night is too much for me to bear. To think what a positive school climate and an engaging classroom climate did for him in the first and second grades was the genesis of my later work and dedication to school climate. Thoughts of how the leadership in that school could allow a teacher like that to continue year after year to destroy the lives of students in a toxic classroom climate consume me at times and drives my motivation to see every school focus on improving school climate.

The third grade was not only disappointing and terrifying, but it was also the first time I realized that adults could be cruel to children. Let me repeat that: It was the first time I realized that adults could be cruel to children – and get away with it. I learned that lesson in school. What a hell of a way and place to learn that lesson.

The question has bothered me for a long time: How could educators allow a teacher like that to work with children? All the teachers in that school and the principal knew what was going on in that classroom and did nothing about it. The principal, who was a kind, caring, jolly person who often visited classrooms, never visited that third-grade class. And the parents of the terrorized students had to see the change at home in their children. The parents had to see their children crying and begging not to go to school. Why did the parents not intervene? They had to know that their children were miserable at school. My parents knew. Parents are key to a school's perception of students.

According to Gallup polls, over 80 percent of the general public believes that support from parents is the most important way to improve the schools, but according to sociological research cited in Malcolm Gladwell's book *Outliers*, economically lower class parents are less likely to be involved in their child's education and are less likely to interact with teachers in the same manner as economically middle and upper-class parents. In other words, they are less likely to participate in a dialogue because they are too often intimidated by the formal setting of a school and because they are more likely to hold the opinion that it is the teacher's responsibility for the education of children and all of the peripheral issues associated with that responsibility (i.e., homework, testing, etc.).

Why is this distinction important? Because decades of research show that when parents are involved in their child's education their children have higher grades; higher test scores; higher graduation rates; better school attendance; increased motivation; higher levels of self-esteem; lower rates of suspension; decreased use of drugs and alcohol; and fewer instances of violent behavior. But parent participation in school is often linked to whether the school climate is negative or positive. In a positive school climate, parents feel welcome and are much more likely to participate in school activities.

Research also shows that schools and school districts that make concentrated and sustained efforts to improve school climate and invite and involve families in the education of their children are more likely to be successful as measured by academic outcomes. Family participation in education is twice as predictive of students' academic success as family socioeconomic status.

By the end of the school year, I was tainted by the third-grade experience. My remaining elementary school experience had highs and lows, but the magic was gone.

Fourth grade was better. After my horrible third grade experience, the matronly fourth-grade teacher was a blessing. She was old but kind, simple but kind, boring but kind, forgetful but kind. Any quirks were acceptable because she was kind. I desperately needed a kind and gentle teacher—each of us that survived the third-grade teacher was desperate for kindness.

Our fourth-grade teacher's quirky habits included her propensity to repeat lessons. At first, we thought she wanted to make sure we understood the lesson, but we later figured out that she forgot that she had already covered the material, so it was repeated. We ended the year well versed in what was then called Long Division because we covered it at least 50 times.

She once sent us out on the playground for recess and apparently forgot about us. The only reason we did not stay on the playground for the entire day we got hungry and came in for lunch. When we all piled back into her class, she looked at us like it was the first day of school. *"I'm so glad you are all here today,"* she said.

We frequently played her version of "Where's Waldo," which was *"Where are the teacher's glasses?"* She lost her glasses at least five times each day. She would say, *"My goodness children, I have mislaid my glasses again. Be darlings and look for them."* Many times, after searching the room for her glasses for several minutes, we would hear a crunching sound signifying that she had found her glasses.

We learned a valuable lesson that year – a group of students have power. We learned that the class bully was nothing but a wimp when faced with several students equally willing to pay him back for years of harassment. Our confidence was born from the fourth-grade teacher's dislike of the bully and her intolerance of his bullying behavior. It started early in the school year when she walked around the corner in the hallway just in time to see the bully twisting a little girl's arm. She lost her glasses again as she beat his butt all the way down the hallway to the principal's office.

After the teacher modeled behavior that bullying would not be tolerated, the class circled the bully each time he tried to pick on another student. The teacher knew exactly what we were doing and ignored the bully's cries for her help. She let us handle the bully, which we did.

All of the good that was restored by our matronly and kind fourth-grade teacher was unraveled by our fifth-grade teacher from Amityville. She intentionally, I'm certain, wore her raven black hair in such a way that it looked like she had horns on her head. She colored her eyebrows dark black to match her horn-rimmed classes. We didn't know where her eyebrows and glasses began and ended. She kept a perpetual snarl on her face and dared students to talk or even ask a question.

The fifth-grade teacher was convinced that boys of the ripe old age of ten were interested in girls in a perverse way. About the only thoughts the boys had about girls at that age was that they talked, walked, and ran funny. She was more concerned about girls being negatively influenced by boys than what quality of education all the students might have access to. Her idea of classroom climate was rigid control and intimidation of boys. She clearly favored girls and tolerated "*you dirty boys*," as she called us.

Psychoanalyst Sigmund Freud could have started a whole new field of psychoanalysis with this teacher. She separated the boys and girls in the classroom into two sections. She put all the girls' desks on one side of the room and the boys' desks on the other side, separated by a path down the middle of the classroom. She seldom sat at her desk. She spent most of her time walking up and down the moral line of demarcation that separated the good from the bad. She kept an evil eye on the boys' side for fear that one of us would break and run to a girl. At lunch, she made certain that all boys sat with each other, far away from the girls. She dared the boys to even look at the girls during recess.

Some might claim the teacher was ahead of her time with gender separation and management by walking around, but she was not that insightful, and her purpose did not relate to the modern-day versions of those concepts. The rationale for her practices was different than that; she was at war with evil–boys.

The teacher made one critical mistake that year which unintentionally served as a relief for all the students. She selected a girl athlete and scholar to read stories to the class each day. This student was more mature, more intelligent, and more insightful than the teacher.

The gifted student read to the girl's half of the room with her back to the boys, as the teacher insisted. It didn't matter. She was an unusually bright student and attractive to 10-year boys because she was also somewhat tomboyish. She was very mature for her age and there was not one student in the class who did not like her. When she read stories, her voice was melodic and soothing, and she had a flair for the perfectly timed dramatic pitch. The teacher even let the student select the stories. They ranged from adventure stories to biographies about great people. She became our surrogate teacher during story time. I learned more from her stories than from anything the teacher covered, and I think most of the other students felt the same way. She was a master of adapting to the whims and weirdness of the classroom and the teacher. She even intervened several times when the teacher was humiliating some unfortunate boy. Her method was to call the teacher's name and say something like, "*I'm sure you want us to cover the math problems at the end of the chapter before we go home today. Isn't that correct?*" The teacher's tirade was interrupted, and the teacher would concede to our saint student friend.

I looked forward to more years and school days with our hero student companion, but the next year she skipped an entire grade. That was unheard of in our little school. She later graduated from high school and college early and became a successful engineer with the United States government where she traveled around the world.

I suppose some students are mature enough with social acumen to survive and thrive in almost any situation. They have an internal drive that allows them to overcome or compensate for poor teaching and a negative school and classroom climate. But those students are rare.

CHAPTER 3
FALLOUT SHELTERS

Fear is that little darkroom where negatives are developed.

-Michael Pritchard

Public education and other issues were overshadowed by the events of the Cuban Missile Crisis in 1962, which was my sixth year in public education.

That was the year I learned that a simple wooden desk could protect children from a nuclear bomb and other evil instruments of Communism. We had to practice emergency drills several times that year that forced every student in the school to huddle under his or her desk for the duration of the drill. We also had to keep our eyes closed. The teachers did not speak to the specific threat except we occasionally saw nuclear explosions on the television. I wasn't the smartest kid around, but I didn't see how our small wooden desks would provide much protection from a nuclear blast.

With the combination of Communistic threats and television, we watched the Cuban Missile Crisis unfold right before our eyes at school with the authoritative voice of Walter Cronkite explaining the circumstances and describing the events. Walter Cronkite was the news; he was mankind's messenger. When Walter Cronkite looked worried, the whole world was worried, especially our teachers. It was not exactly comforting to hear your teacher muttering, *"They're going to do it; they're going to do it"* repeatedly as CBS News showed pictures of warships on a map of the Atlantic Basin. We weren't exactly sure who was going to do what, but we were bright enough to figure out that it had something to do with the sturdiness of our desks and the possibility of very bright lights in the sky. There are adults who lived through the nuclear threat era of the 1960s that probably have a wooden desk in their basements just in case we experience another nuclear threat.

That year I learned that not all people in my small community relied on wooden desks to shield them from the coming nuclear holocaust. My Sunday school teacher, who also happened to be the Baptist minister at my church and a substitute teacher at my school, invited his Sunday school class over to his house one beautiful late fall afternoon shortly after the end of the Cuban Missile Crisis. We frolicked in his backyard, ate grilled hamburgers, drank quarts of Kool-Aid, and visited the minister's nuclear fallout shelter.

The kids were more than a little confused when the God-fearing, pillar-of-faith, leader-of-the-community, bigger-than-life minister took us down a dark, creepy concrete stairwell into an underground bunker that was the size of a bedroom. He made it clear that this was not a bunker; it was a "fallout shelter." It was stocked with canned foods, bottled Cokes, a ham radio, huge containers of water, magazines, books, a weird little chemical port-o-potty, and a Bible. He proceeded to tell us that being ten feet underground would protect him and his wife from the thermonuclear blast when the nuclear missiles hit Atlanta and the military bases in and near Atlanta (Ft. McPherson, Ft. Gilliam, Dobbins Air Force Base)-all strategic targets of the Soviet Union's military. Even though our community was miles from these targets, the minister explained something called collateral damage–our community would suffer collateral damage.

As he explained the rationale for his fallout shelter, the good minister stated that everyone above ground would die a horrible death, either from radiation burns or gut-wrenching radiation poisoning. He said, "*Do you kids know what radiation poisoning does to a person?*" We collectively shook our heads no, which encouraged him to give a graphic description that he must have found in *Radiation Today* magazine. He reassured us, however, that because we lived near so many "target-rich" areas, we would probably not feel a thing. Our death would be quick and painless–something about being vaporized.

He said that he and his wife had practiced evacuating from their bedroom to the fallout shelter. He added proudly, "*We can make it to safety in three minutes or less.*" One of the kids asked, "*Why don't you practice evacuating from other parts of the house?*" The wise man-of-God said, "*Everyone knows the Communists will slip their missiles over the horizon in the dark, in the middle of the night; that's how Communists think.*"

As if I did not have enough to worry about in the dark of night already, now here is a minister telling us that an unnamed, unmanned missile of total destruction will appear one night, and we will wake up vaporized. The real message was this: God will not help the masses; he will help the ministers of the world who have a fallout shelter.

There was one other question from the group of doomed children standing in the middle of a fallout shelter while the birds were singing above ground: "*Why can't we come to your fallout shelter when the Communist fire their missiles at us?"* The quick, sharp, and clipped answer from the minister was, *"Because there is only enough room and food for two of us."* My friend Jess said, *"Didn't Jesus feed the multitudes with a fish and loaf of bread?"* *"This ain't Sunday school, kids. Let's go drink some Kool-Aid,"* said the minister of the Gospel. We spent the rest of the afternoon looking toward the sky.

We never visited the minister's fallout shelter again and when I told my parents about the fallout shelter they looked at each other in that way parents do that says without words: *"Oh, crap, how do we explain this one to him so he won't have nightmares for a month?"*

Both are scary thoughts - being vaporized by a nuclear blast from the Communists in the middle of the night or having to spend months locked in a fallout shelter with the minister.

CHAPTER 4
FROM SCHOOL PRAYER TO WORKPLACE

Stupidity does not give way to science, technology, modernity, progress; on the contrary, it progresses right along with progress.

-Milan Kundera

In one of those ironies in history, just when we needed to pray that either the desks could really withstand a nuclear blast or that the Soviet missiles would run out of fuel before they reached the United States or that the minister could fit thousands of worshippers into his fallout shelter, the 1962 United States Supreme Court ruled that prayer cannot be forced in public schools. With all due respect to the High Court, there were probably more prayers in schools in 1962 than before or since.

The Court decision, as was the case with most Supreme Court decisions, was met with little interest in my community and school, other than when the same minister proclaimed, "*I'd like to see them come take prayer out of our schools – the Communists,*" which was greeted with "*Amen, brother*" throughout the church.

During those times, anything and everything bad was because of the Communists. The Supreme Court was filled with Communists, according to the local gossip at the country store, school, and church. Joseph McCarthy was dead and gone but the memory of this Red Scare lingered on in the Deep South. McCarthy fabricated accusations, but according to a few believers, he was "*probably on to something.*"

So, despite the United States Supreme Court's decision to take prayer out of schools, daily prayer in my school continued. Each school day was started with either a prayer or a reading of Scripture.

The other peculiarity of the sixth grade was what teachers kept referring to as the "New Math." The name was given to a set of teaching practices introduced in the United States shortly after the Sputnik crisis in order to boost scientific education and mathematical skill in the population so that the intellectual threat of Soviet engineers, reputedly skilled mathematicians, could be met. In other words, the United States was in a panic because the Soviet Union had moved ahead.

This New Math looked pretty much like the old math to the students in my small school. Math still had numbers and function symbols. There may have been a few more word problems, but that didn't fool anybody. It was just math hidden in a sentence or paragraph. What we did not know and could not have known is that we did not have New Math, we were still being taught old math because the New Math required significant teacher training and the introduction of Math Theory. Many school districts did not have the means or funding to train teachers, so they simply ignored New Math. It's probably a good thing to ignore public education fads, and this was no exception because soon after New Math was introduced, Morris Kline wrote a book, "*Why Johnny Can't Read: The Failure of New Math*," that was a scathing critique of the failure of New Math. Students were learning about "set theory" but could not do multiplication.

All this turmoil and debate had no impact on our school or teachers. The students thought the New Math probably had something to do with the Cuban Missile Crisis, and I'm certain our minister expected to see New Math books written in Russian.

At that time, Raymond Callahan had all the answers to public education's problems and the budding threat of a Communist takeover. The National Defense Education Act pumped money into and placed an emphasis on public education on the heels of the Soviet Union Sputnik launch.

Raymond Callahan stepped forward to put public education back on the right path, or so he said. Callahan, a successful businessman, wrote *Education and the Cult of Efficiency*. He argued that if public education operated like a business the outcomes would be greatly improved and the Soviet Union would not be intellectually and scientifically ahead of the United States. Callahan advocated applying business principles, values and practices to public education in a cult-like manner.

This was an interesting argument because in the same year his book was published, *Time* magazine reported 15,782 business failures for the year with lost assets of over $1.2 billion. According to *Time* magazine, 91.3 percent of the business failures were due to business principles, values, practices of management, and a negative work-place climate. Nevertheless, Callahan's book led to many educational changes across the nation—most of which either did not last or were never fully implemented. That is typically the way with fads.

Several times during the last century and even today, business-type people and business-like people believe with sincerity and good intentions that public and private education should be operated like a business even though there exists no evidence that business practices are effective in education settings.

Since many people believe that all organizations should operate as a business, let's take a closer look at what that really means. According to *Forbes*, eight out of every 10 new businesses fail within the first 18 months. There is an average of 15,000 business failures per year in the United States. Which business model do the business advocates want schools to use? Which company business model do people want schools to adopt?

The overgeneralizations about running all organizations like a business run up against the data and facts. Instead of relying solely on a business model, leaders should first consider what is best for the organization and how their behavior and decision-making can benefit the organization. The strategic plan should be an operational plan that remains true to the purpose and nature of the organization instead of being forced into a model that may not be suitable. And every organization must understand the importance of workplace climate.

So much of the importance of workplace climate is linked to human motivation and the elements that motivate people. Motivation is what causes people to act. It is the process that moves people to meet their needs, react to challenges, respond to fear, and drives them to engage with others or a task.

The field of organizational psychology has for many years addressed the culture and climate of the workplace and its dynamic effect on employee morale, productivity, and retention. Many of the business turnaround models and strategies and the stories of these successful efforts have and continue to focus on changing or improving the workplace culture and climate, which in turn affects the behavior and productivity of employees and others that interact with the climate.

Thompson and Luthans offer seven characteristics of culture and climate in the workplace.

1. *Culture equals behavior.*
2. *Culture is learned.*
3. *Climate is learned through interaction.*
4. *Subcultures form through rewards.*
5. *People shape the culture and climate.*
6. *Culture is negotiated.*
7. *Culture and climate are difficult to change.*

According to Thompson and Luthan, people in the workplace learn and adopt behavior that they are exposed to on a regular basis – *negative* or *positive*. How employees interact with each other is often determined by how the supervisors interact with the employees, and that interaction has the "subordinate effect" – where behavior and attitude (negative or positive) are pushed out through the ranks of the organization, creating a workplace climate that results in comradeship and mutual support in the organization or has a deleterious impact on employees and eventually the organization. The negative impact on employees can be the genesis of subcultures. Subcultures are present in every organization. They can be productive or destructive. According to Sackman,

Subcultures form when a group of people within an organization share a situation, problem, or experience that is unique to them.

Organizational psychology models explain how subcultures are created in organizations.

All individuals have needs and some of the basic needs are belonging, interacting, and receiving feedback from others. If a person does not feel like he belongs and only interacts with a small number of colleagues or friends, and there is either no feedback or negative feedback from supervisors or other colleagues, the person feels driven to find a group of like individuals. Then a subculture is born. These subcultures can over time undermine the strength of the organization if the collective attitude of the subculture becomes anti-organization. Another way of explaining this is to understand the relationship between culture and climate: culture is the behavior of people in the organization and climate is why they behave that way. This applies to any type of organization or institution.

Many of the organizational psychology components are reflective of Albert Bandura's work in social psychology. Bandura developed the *Triadic Responsibility Model* that triangulated overt behavior, personal factors, and the environment. The environment component of the triad includes the surroundings of the individual that stimulates, stifles, or otherwise influences the behavior and attitude of individuals. Bandura's theory is referred to as *reciprocal determinism*:

Reciprocal determinism suggests that individuals' function because of dynamic and reciprocal interaction among their behavior, environment, and personal characteristics. Personal characteristics include one's thoughts, emotions, expectations, beliefs, goals, and so forth. Behavior is conceptualized as a person's skills and actions. Lastly, the environment is a person's social and physical surroundings. All three systems interact with one another; therefore, a change in one will influence the others as well. Reciprocal determinism indicates that people do have a say in their future, because of reciprocal interactions.

Reciprocal interactions suggest that altering a person's environment can trigger significant changes in his personal characteristics and behavior.

According to Jeff Blair, based on his work on workplace climate, an organization's human resources department (HRD) must take on the role of a "*strategic climate partner.*" They should assist line managers to create positive workplace climates to attract and retain employees. In the school setting, this role falls on school leadership–the principal and assistant principals. A positive school climate begins with leadership. To do this, leaders must understand these critically important points.

1. *There is a correlation between a negative or inconsistent climate and employees' abilities to do their jobs effectively.*
2. *Managers should be trained to recognize warning signs or concerns related to changes in an employee's behaviors or attitudes that can negatively affect the climate and the productivity of employees around the person.*
3. *Managers must be capable of recognizing factors that can alter the environment in positive or negative ways.*

Workplace climate is the health and atmosphere of the workplace. Just as atmospheric conditions can affect daily activities, workplace climate can impact behavior at work. A positive workplace climate can improve employee's work habits and a negative workplace climate can impede good work habits and problem-solving. A positive workplace climate leads to and sustains staff motivation, higher performance, safety, and employee retention. When people work in a positive workplace climate, they seek to produce results and they interact effectively and efficiently with their colleagues.

A study of several corporations found that a positive workplace climate accounted for almost 33 percent of profits, efficiency, and revenue growth. The study of 2,500 organizational units in 24 organizations reported in the Harvard Business Review, found further that the importance of a positive workplace climate exceeded the effects of pay and benefits. The study also found that the manager working closest to the employees had the most direct impact on the workplace climate for the employees. These findings point out the importance of workplace climate in all settings, including schools. If top leaders stress the importance of workplace climate then managers throughout the organization are more likely to also focus on a positive workplace climate.

Research conducted and reported by *Management Sciences for Health* found several important factors to remember about positively influencing workplace climate. These factors are instrumental when developing and evaluating workplace climate strategies; in fact, they are important in any type of workplace, including schools because they reflect the basic elements that can make the climate of a facility either negative or positive. These are elements that leaders should recognize and observe on a regular basis.

The following matrix provides details about each factor.

Get to know the staff better.	Leaders at every level of the organization need to take time to learn more about employees. This benefits communications and is early detection of morale or other problems.
Focus on clarifying expectations and identifying challenges.	Employees work in a state of anxiety if their immediate supervisor has not established expectations and is not cognizant of employees' challenges.
Lead the entire team around shared goals and aspirations.	Leaders need to focus on a common and shared agenda for all employees to create a sense of teamwork. Shared goals and aspirations build stronger teams.
Mobilize individuals by addressing their needs for power, affiliation, or achievement.	All employees have needs that are basic to their attitude in the workplace. Some are motivated by recognition while others strive on increasing levels of responsibility and opportunities of affiliation with other employees.
Inspire team members by recognizing their accomplishments and modeling the kind of behavior you seek in others.	The leader must always recognize that employees are watching and learning, which means many of them will emulate the behavior and attitude of leaders while at the same time looking for feedback and recognition for a job well done or constructive criticism.

The same research found that an organization can improve workplace climate when other functions and practices invite participation, such as planning regular meetings to exchange information on progress, shared learning, effective management experiences, and success. When colleagues share information on a regular basis, it promotes work efficiency and information flow, and it advocates implementing activities that move employees toward shared goals, monitored progress, and using mistakes as sources for learning.

A Gallup Poll showed that, even when workplaces offered benefits such as flextime and work-from-home opportunities, employees preferred workplace well-being and a positive work environment to material benefits.

A *Harvard Business Review* study found that well-being comes from one place, and one place only—a positive climate. All the elements of a positive workplace climate apply to school climate. Successful businesses and successful schools have many things in common, but the most influential is a positive climate. So, there *is* a business model that would work in schools; it's called workplace climate.

CHAPTER 5
SAFETY PATROL AND LOST INNOCENCE

Everything happens for a reason; if you can't find a reason for something, there's a reason for that.

-Chris Levi

In 1963 I'm not certain which event had the most compelling influence on the world of public education—me being named a safety patrol in my elementary school or the pronouncement by the National Council for Teachers of English (NCTE) that *"The study of grammar does not benefit writing."* A collective "amen" was heard across America from students struggling to remember the eight parts of speech. With this denunciation of grammar, I thought the dictates of the Supreme Court and the Communist threat were over and God was back in business-prayers were being answered.

The logic of the NCTE was formed around "free-flow thinking and writing." In other words, all that grammar stuff was getting in the way of thinking and creating. Now I could explain to my parents why my grades in English were so bad. All the grammar crap was interrupting my keen sense of free-flowing thoughts. However, my hopes were quickly dashed because most English teachers across America did not share my view or the position of the NCTE regarding grammar, and again a public education fad crashed and burned.

The public's perception of public education during the grammar war became even more clouded by anthropologist Jules Henry's assault on public education that same year. In his book *Culture against Man*, Henry questioned educational institutions. According to Henry, the purpose of school is to cultivate an endearment of the culture in America instead of encouraging free thought, the world view of cultures, or the importance of education as a tool for man's advancement. The author seemed angry about America's economic structure, values, parent-child relationships, teenage issues, old age, and just about everything else in America. He just seemed angry. Apparently, schools in America were the cause of many of its woes, according to Henry. Henry's book not only echoed a growing concern about public education, but it also brought psychologists, social workers, and anthropologists into the public education discussion.

While Callahan was advocating business principles, the NCTE was advocating grammar-less education, and New Math was the path to world supremacy, human and social service professionals like Henry claimed that public education was minimizing education and producing the robots that Callahan said were needed to make schools functionally successful and important to society. Henry opined that the education focus was contrary to America's basic principles.

At the same time the great debates were taking place in 1963 about public education, another critically important event took place. I was selected to be on my elementary school's safety patrol squad, a great honor. I was never very clear about the reason for my selection to this elite group. I was not a good student academically. I was not a gifted athlete, and I was not much to look at. Regardless of how it happened, it did and I'm sure the shock was felt around the world. At the time, I thought it was the school's way of apologizing for my third and fifth-grade teachers.

This is how it happened. One day I was pulled out of class and sent to the principal's office. Expecting the worse, of course, I was mentally preparing myself with all the staple excuses of childhood: "*I didn't mean to;*" "*It wasn't my fault;*" "*They made me do it.*" As I waited in the outer office, I witnessed a parade of smart, nice looking and popular students coming into the principal's office area. I did not want them to see me there or hear me scream when the principal skinned me alive for something I probably did. They chatted away with me and each other as if they were used to being sent to the principal's office for good deeds, which they were. [It occurred to me that all these students were in the other third and fifth-grade teachers' classrooms and were therefore shielded from the witches I had to contend with.]

The students were perfectly comfortable in the principal's office. The principal appeared at his doorway with a remarkably bright smile and greeted each of the other students with a handshake and invitation to his office. I just sat there thankful I had more time to figure out which transgression I was going to be punished for so that I could appropriately select the best excuse. But then the principal said, "Garry, come in." Oh, my God, a firing squad! The most popular, gifted, and best-looking kids in the school were going to be witnesses and participates in my execution. I walked in with my head down. I expected the worse type of fate—embarrassment. Embarrassment or the fear of such rules the world of children and adults. So many decisions are made, usually bad decisions, because of the fear of embarrassment. Some students will knowingly misbehave to get kicked out of class to avoid embarrassment. Adults will hide or skip important events to avoid potentially embarrassing moments.

To my complete shock, the principal told me and ten other students that we were selected to be on the safety patrol squad. You must understand that this was a place of honor, a distinction of pride, a selection that could raise one's place in the social strata of the school. We were given shiny metal law enforcement-type badges and a hardness type belt that we wore when on duty.

The duties of a safety patrol were essentially to stand in the hallway and tell kids to be quiet, tell kids to quit playing football in the bathroom, to make sure the little kindergarten and first grade kids did not get on the wrong bus, and to make sure kids did not throw things at each other before and after school.

When I returned to class with my badge, the teacher made a big event of my selection. He talked about dependability, hard work, and "anything is possible." He seemed to focus a lot on that last point. But I did not care – I was somebody. I had an identity. My parents were equally proud and surprised. I performed my safety patrol duties with pride and miraculously my grades improved. It must have been the badge's magical powers.

The duties of the safety patrols took a totally unexpected turn one day in the autumn of 1963. While students were on the playground on a clear, cold November day, panicked-stricken teachers suddenly interrupted our play and hastily ushered all students back into the school. We did not go back to our classrooms; instead, we were huddled into the small school cafeteria that also served as an auditorium. The principal stood on the stage and announced in grave tones that President J.F. Kennedy had been shot. Teachers were crying and the kids were watching the teachers and each other – fully oblivious to what this all meant. In the minds and hearts of the students what the principal said made no sense. Certainly, the President of the United States cannot be mortal. Someone that important cannot be shot. Even though we didn't quite comprehend the gravity of what was taking place, fear and sorrow hung in the air, especially fear. After the principal's announcement, we all went to our classrooms.

One thing to remember about elementary students that is extremely different than middle school or high school students is that young students look to their teachers for a reaction and they tend to mirror the teachers' reaction to difficult events while middle and high school students usually don't care how a teacher reacts.

On this day, students cried because teachers cried not because we understood what happened. After the principal's brief report of the event, we headed back to our respective classes and teachers were told to keep the classroom doors closed. The condition of the president was unknown and the circumstances surrounding the shooting were unfolding, so many classrooms that day turned into prayer rooms.

In the early afternoon, the school's static-laced intercom summoned all safety patrols to the principal's office. In the compact principal's office was a tiny television set on a small table. The principal had his back to us when we entered his office. He tried to gather himself before he turned around to face us. With red eyes, tears streaming down his face and a small voice, he told us to watch history taking place. I looked around the room, taking in everything about this office and the people standing there. The principal, his secretary, the custodian, and one teacher were standing there with the safety patrols, eyes transfixed on Walter Cronkite. Again, there was the voice of mankind trying to guide the world through yet another crisis. Later generations will never understand the power and influence of Walter Cronkite. His was the soothing voice in tragic times; he was the one voice that said everything will be okay; he was the voice we could all trust and depend on; he was the voice of reason; he was the voice of America.

A few minutes later, fighting tears, Walter Cronkite shocked the world and our small gathering in the principal's office with the news that President Kennedy was dead. The principal turned away for a moment and everyone else in the room cried softly. I did not grasp the moment. My kid's mind was still trying to reconcile my minister's lack of faith in God and now I learn that even a president is not safe. What hope does a little kid have in this type of world? How could a little kid survive?

The principal collected himself and said he wanted the safety patrols to go to each classroom and call the teacher out to the hallway and tell them about President Kennedy's death. He did not want to make such a grave announcement over the intercom. I liked the principal, and I think he was a good man, but what sense did it make to send young kids who were still in a state of shock and fear, to tell teachers that one of the biggest and most heartbreaking tragedies in United States history had taken place—to tell adults that President Kennedy was dead?

My assignment was to tell the seventh-grade teachers. After telling only one teacher, the rest of the teachers spilled out into the hallways and the day turned into emotional turmoil. To my knowledge, none of the teachers or the principal considered the trauma and fear going through all the students.

In a positive school climate, the concerns of the students would have been foremost on the minds of the teachers. The teachers would have engaged in reassuring students that there was nothing to fear. Instead, the teachers were in the hallways while the students were left in the classrooms.

The teachers did not know how to react or what to do. Time in schools across America on that day stood still. Teachers and other adults in the schools were overcome with emotion and students were terrified, mystified, and traumatized by the death of the president and the lack of engagement by the teachers. No adults tried to reassure the students that everything would be okay.

Our school released early that day. I remember watching the students board school buses with the look of victims on their young faces.

For me and some of my friends, comfort and understanding that day came from our school bus driver, of all people, and not the teachers. When we all filed quietly onto the school bus, the students sat down in their seats and did not talk or even look around. Our bus driver pulled away from the school but shortly thereafter he slowly guided the school bus into an empty church parking lot. I thought he was too upset to drive. However, he stood up and turned around to talk to us. He stood there as tall and strong as a tree and looked us over. He said simply and softly, *"Listen. Sometimes bad things happen that make kids afraid. This is one of those times. President Kennedy was a good man and he was killed by a bad man, but you will be okay, and the world will be okay. It is okay to cry and this is one of those times when it's okay for your teachers and parents to cry because it's a sad time. But don't be afraid. It's okay to be sad, but don't be afraid."* Here was an adult who knew something about kids. Kids are okay unless they are afraid. That point is not covered in most teacher preparation classes and is often overlooked in all aspects of public education and on people that work with children. Trauma comes primarily from fear. Kids need to be reassured. A positive school climate focuses on reducing fear and increasing assurances and security of emotions.

Playing the role of the grim reaper notwithstanding, I otherwise enjoyed my new status as a safety patrol until I threw the school bully headfirst into the school's flag pole. He was picking on a little third grader. I figured the poor third grader had enough to deal with and being bullied at the end of the day was too much for anybody.

I did not mean to ram the bully into the flag pole—I really did not. After all, the flag pole was a symbol of pride to me, because I was the safety patrol responsible for running up and bringing down the United States and state flags each day. It just so happens that when I yanked him away from his third-grade victim, my momentum took the bully flying past me and right into the flag pole head first. Wham! I think that flag pole is still vibrating from the collision. The aftermath of the incident is representative of justice in America for kids. The third grader is ridiculed for being the victim; I was removed from safety patrol duty; and the bully is pampered and consoled just because he's bleeding from his forehead. Another lesson about adults— be the last to get hurt and it clears all previous misdeeds. The bullying victim was humiliated, and I lost all interest in school when I turned in my safety patrol badge. Maybe I cried, but I don't remember–humiliation and injustice do something to our memory.

CHAPTER 6
SEVENTH GRADE PSYCHOSIS

I am not strange; I am just not normal.

-Salvador Dali

Our small rural school started growing very quickly with the rapid increase in new and affordable housing in our community. By the time I reached the seventh grade, we had five seventh grade teachers, each with a distinct personality. In previous years the school only had two seventh grade teachers.

Public education does indeed include a cast of characters. The primary purpose of the seventh grade in that era was to prepare students for high school, which meant learning how to adjust to different teachers and changing classes several times each day for different subjects, just like we were expected to do in high school. The whole exercise of adjusting to changing classes was not really related to a change in routine, it was learning how to adjust to the different psychological conditions of more than one teacher and the different climates of classrooms.

Until the seventh grade, students were stuck with and had to adapt to only one saint or witch all day. But in the seventh grade, students had to learn to adapt to several different personalities in five different classrooms, plus each of the five teachers had a different substitute teacher. So, that makes 10 possible personalities to adjust to. I can see why kids needed that seventh-grade experience to prepare them for the emotional rigors of middle or high school.

We did not anticipate, however, that some teachers would have multiple personalities. One of my seventh-grade teachers I am certain suffered from acute stress disorder, anxiety disorder, avoidant personality disorder and probably other disorders. At first, she appeared to be quick and efficient, but a closer look showed that she was not quick but nervous, not efficient but compulsive. Ten minutes into class and she had tears in her eyes; twenty minutes into class and she was in the back corner of the room with her back turned toward the class murmuring something unintelligible. One time while using an overhead projector, she started drawing little circles on the plastic cover without explanation. It was entertaining for a few minutes to see her psychosis displayed on the screen in front of the darkened room in the form of meaningless little circles, but after a while, it became downright spooky.

According to the experts, a histrionic personality disorder is characterized by a person who is always calling attention to himself or herself and being overly dramatic. When the person is overly dramatic, minor situations can cause wild swings in emotions. Also, this type of person, according to the Diagnostic and Statistical Manual (DSM), is easily bored with normal routines and craves new, novel situations and excitement. In relationships, they form bonds quickly, but the relationships are often shallow, with the person demanding increasing amounts of attention.

Welcome to the histrionic world of my seventh grade Social Studies teacher. He was off the wall most days and very entertaining. He never took attendance roll and painted pictures on the window blinds so that when he opened and closed them, they made a primitive moving cartoon of people. He proclaimed that his current job was paying the bills until his acting career took off. His mood swings ranged from splendid class discussions and illustrations to dark, brooding epistles about life. He once spent an entire class period playing the various roles of characters from Hamlet. That was somewhat entertaining for a few minutes, but during most of the class time we talked to each other. I think he was into Hamlet's soliloquy when class ended.

While the Social Studies teacher was histrionic, at least he wasn't paranoid like our Physical Education (PE) teacher. The teacher acted like we were plotting something each minute of each day. We were no threat; we were too stupid to plot anything. We were just trying to get through the nuclear era without getting vaporized and wondering what was for lunch. Nevertheless, Mr. PE treated the kids like guilty cretins. Yelling and screaming about trying to undermine his authority and talking about him behind his back was a daily accusation. He even accused us of deflating the basketballs and footballs on purpose and sabotaging this new game called tetherball.

We didn't do much to the basketballs and footballs, but we did sabotage the tetherball rope because it was the dumbest game adults every created to torture kids. What joy can kids have standing one on each side of a tall pole hitting a soccer-type ball tethered to a rope back and forth until one kid overpowers the other kid and causes the rope to wrap around the pole all the way up to the top? Sometimes the weaker kid would get strapped to the pole by the rope traveling the speed of light as the ball circumnavigated the pole and the kid.

I saw the power of expectations evolve in the PE teacher's class. He expected the kids to talk about him behind his back, so eventually we did. He expected the kids to let the air out of the basketballs and footballs, so eventually we did—we even exceeded his expectations by hiding the PE equipment and supplies in the trees that surrounded the playground. But our proudest moment came when we shorten the tetherball rope each afternoon a little at a time. By the end of my seventh-grade year, the PE teacher had good reason to be paranoid; we were out to get him.

In fairness, most of my seventh-grade teachers were wonderful, and one was an angel even though she made us do the very unnatural thing of diagramming sentences. If it was not unnatural, at least it was archaic. How archaic? Most methods of diagramming sentences are based on the work of Alonzo Reed and Brainerd Kellogg in their book *Higher Lessons in English*, first published in 1877. Reed and Kellogg were preceded by, and their work probably informed by, W. S. Clark, who published his "balloon" method of depicting grammar in his 1847 book *A Practical Grammar: In Which Words, Phrases & Sentences are Classified According to Their Offices and Their Various Relationships to Each Another*. The 1800s—that's how archaic. We were doing non-sense that was outdated by a hundred years. Where were the quirky public education fads when we needed them? The reaction of kids to any announcement that diagramming sentences was the next assignment was met with the same type of moaning and complaining typically reserved for tetherball. Even though we liked the teacher, she was stuck in the 19th century with most things. This was an English teacher who had a dartboard on her bulletin board with "NTCE" (National Council of English Teachers) in the center.

Regardless of her occasional fall from grace during her diagrammatic blackouts, she was an excellent teacher. She ran a well-planned classroom with a positive climate and no wasted time or effort. We were put to work as soon as we walked in the classroom and we were engaged in work until the bell rang to signal the change of classes. In today's public education world that is called "engagement." She told us what we were going to study, how we were going to study it, and at the end of the class period, she told us what we had studied and what we were going to study the next day. For students, there was security and reassurance in her orderliness and a sense of belonging because of her encouragement. We received a significant dose of encouragement each day. Instead of a big red-letter grade on your paper, for example, she would write a note about what was good and then she would write what needed more work. She always added: "*Let me know if you need help.*" We looked forward to her class.

How did she handle discipline problems? We did not have time to be a discipline problem. She kept our education moving; she always kept the classroom climate positive. She kept us engaged in the learning process. We felt cared for and connected. We learned subject matter, but we also got a glimpse of how to study, how to prepare for a test, how to work with each other, how to utilize our strengths, when to ask for help, and even how to take a test.

To further illustrate the wonderful heart of the teacher, several years later after she moved to another state she heard that one of her former elementary students was killed in action in Viet Nam, she came to the funeral.

The substitute teachers did not suffer from any discernable psychological disorders. There is surprisingly little research considering how important and prevalent substitute teachers are in public education. However, a study released by the Center for American Progress, *Tales of Teacher Absence: New Research Yields Patterns that Speak to Policymakers,* reports that *"Every school day approximately five percent of teachers will be absent from school and replaced by a substitute."*

The high number of absences costs districts millions of dollars annually in substitute teacher pay and takes a toll on student learning, the report noted. The study found that teachers are typically absent nine or ten days per year. That means that between kindergarten and 12th grade, students are taught by someone other than their primary teacher for the equivalent of *two-thirds of a school year.* Add teacher absenteeism to the issues related to the quality of substitute teaching plus student absences and the impact on student achievement is enormous. Therefore, the issues related to substitute teachers are significant.

According to an article by Chris Mikesell,

Taking care of substitute teaching in a district is in many ways like taking care of a beautiful garden. It is easy to see how the elements of a garden like the soil and the plants can compare with the district environment and the substitute teachers themselves. To achieve success, both gardens must be cared for with diligence and knowledge.

Most substitute teachers I had were blandly insignificant. But substitute teaching is a thankless job, no doubt, and there are thousands of excellent substitute teachers. There are some, however, that should do anything but teach.

As a student in public schools, I had literally dozens of substitute teachers. Most of them were harmless, but those school days with substitute teachers were typically wasted days. I viewed them as a welcomed day of goofing off, but usually the classroom would be in chaos before the morning was over and it was not uncommon for the principal to show up in class to tell everybody to behave. I also remember having a substitute teacher for several days at a time because the regular teacher was out sick. While one day with a substitute teacher might be okay, it was agony to have a substitute teacher for two or more days. It meant a disruptive classroom, bored students, and a stack of worksheets (busy work) day after day. Then when the regular teacher returned, she would almost always say something like, "*What have you been doing?*" And then she would chastise us on how badly we behaved, based on the substitute teacher's report.

As I mentioned, there were a few exceptional substitute teachers, and there were a few so eccentric that the students loved to have them in class. One comes to mind when I was in high school. He was the best of them all. He was an elderly man - tall, thin with a thick crop of bright white hair that was always unruly. He walked with a slight limp and he slumped forward when he sat in a chair or on a stool. He had sky blue eyes and an elegantly aristocratic air about him, which stood him apart from everyone else in the school and the community. He had a southern aristocratic accent with a hint of old New Orleans. He wore a bowtie and a white crumpled suit each time he substituted for an English teacher, and he had the same routine whether it was an Honors English class or the dregs of the school, like my class. He became legendary throughout the school. He carried a Carl Sandburg book of poems into the classroom. He sat on a stool at the front of the class and read Carl Sandburg poems all class period regardless of what the students were doing, even if they were misbehaving, which seldom happened.

Imagine a classroom like mine filled with high school students who had very little if any interest in school, who attended school because they had to and because it was the most convenient way to socialize. Think of a class of students that one teacher referred to as "a collection of thugs and losers." Imagine that class being enthralled by an elderly man reading Carl Sandberg poems for an entire class period. How was that possible? How could he hold the attention of this class without even trying? This was the same class that was notorious for running off substitute teachers.

What I remember most, other than the elderly man's appearance and accent, was his total immersion into his reading of the poems. He read the poems with drama, with enthusiasm, with flare. He loved what he was doing, and he always reminded us that he knew Carl Sandburg and met him each year when Sandburg made a stop at Agnes Scott College (an academically acclaimed small, private college in Decatur, Georgia) as Sandburg migrated to his winter home in Florida. For the first time in a long time, or for some students in that class it may have been the only time, we witnessed a teacher who loved what he was doing, and it affected the classroom climate. The poetry content mattered to him; it was his passion and, in that passion, and love for what he was doing he brought us along for the ride.

That is in fact what good teachers do. They do not teach to teach; they share their love of the subject. One afternoon, the class cheered after he read Sandberg's "*To a Dead Man*,"

Over the deadline, we have called to you
To come across with a word to us
Some beaten whisper of what happens
Where you are over the deadline
Deaf to our calls and voiceless.

The flickering shadows have not answered
Nor your lips sent a signal
Whether love talks and roses grow
And the sun breaks in the morning
Splattering the sea with crimson.

He read it with passion, with his whole heart. He came off of the stool, dropped the book to his side and recited from memory the last stanza. Wow—that was impressive and powerful. He was a substitute teacher who was not a substitute. He was the real thing.

CHAPTER 7
EIGHT PARTS OF SPEECH OR DEATH

If at first, you don't succeed, failure may be your style.

-Quentin Crisp

My most creditable friends, the ones with siblings already in high school, warned me that I would probably be killed in high school. I would be tortured and publicly humiliated, or at best I would have my head stuck in a toilet and flushed. By whom and for what reason was never clearly stated so I wasn't sure whether to keep an eye on other kids or on the teachers when I entered high school.

In those days, middle schools did not exist in most states. Middle schools were created by people who thought six and seventh-grade students needed to be prepared for the rigors of high school and eighth graders needed to be protected from the older students in high school. Or, maybe someone thought it was a good idea to put a bunch of very immature students together in a school where the sixth-grade boys are about half the size of eighth-grade girls and where eighth-grade students were in leadership roles to harass and intimidate and bully sixth and seventh-grade students every day without impunity. The concept was to "protect" immature students from the rabble in high school. Educators created a whole new world and a unique type of misery for pre-adolescents and early-adolescents.

The public education decision to create middle schools was made without a modicum of research supporting the concept. In fact, much of the research today shows that middle schools are an academic wasteland, are incubators for bullying behavior, and when the first thoughts of dropping out of school enter a student's thoughts, probably because whatever nurturing a student experienced in elementary school is gone and because students are thinking if high school is worse than this, then they will start working on an exit strategy in middle school.

In an article for the American School Board Journal, Lawrence Hardy wrote: *"Dropping out is a process, not a single act, and students who will eventually drop out send distress signals for years -- that is, at least as far back as middle school."* Hardy quotes Gail Hilliard-Nelson, director of the New Jersey Consortium for Middle Schools, who said, *"If they don't physically drop out in middle school they mentally drop out."*

In his compelling article about the challenges and the importance of middle school, Hardy cites the work of Balfanz and Letgers who found in a study of Philadelphia's dropouts that there are four indicators that can cause a sixth-grader to later drop out: a final grade of F in math and English, attendance below 80 percent for the year, and a final "unsatisfactory" behavior mark in at least one class. Having just one of these indicators gave a sixth-grader a three-in-four chance of dropping out of high school. Students with more than one indicator had an even higher dropout rate over the next six years.

Researchers at the University of Michigan studied the transition from elementary to middle school and found that:

1. *On average, children's grades drop dramatically during the first year of middle school compared to their grades in elementary school.*
2. *After moving to middle school, children become less interested in school and less self-assured about their abilities.*
3. *Compared to elementary schools, middle schools are more controlling, less cognitively challenging and focus more on competition and comparing students' ability.*

According to the American Psychological Association,

Psychologists discovered a 'developmental mismatch' between the environment and philosophy of middle schools and the children they attempt to teach. At a time when children's cognitive abilities are increasing, middle school offers students fewer opportunities for decision-making and lower levels of cognitive involvement, but a more complex social environment. At the same time, numerous teachers have replaced the single classroom teacher and students often face larger classes and a new group of peers. These factors all interact to make the transition to middle school difficult for many youngsters. Studies find the decreased motivation and self-assuredness contribute to poor academic performance; poor grades trigger more self-doubt and a downward spiral can begin.

The wisdom (or lack thereof) of the middle school concept from the student and parent perspective was captured in a *Time Magazine* article.

It is 10 a.m. on a bright sunny day in May and the Fine Arts wing at Gustav A. Fritsche Middle School in Milwaukee, Wisconsin, is hopping. In a band room, 21 members of the jazz ensemble are rehearsing Soul Bossa Nova with plenty of heart and impressive intonation, in preparation for a concert downtown. In another room, woodblocks, timpani, and bells are whipping up a rhythmic frenzy as the 75-member Fritsche Philharmonic Orchestra tackles Elliott Del Borgo's Aboriginal Rituals. In an art room, eighth-graders are shaping clay vessels to be baked in the school kiln. Down the hall, students are dabbing acrylic paints on canvas to create vivid still life's à la Vincent van Gogh. At 10:49, when the 82-minute arts period ends, kids of all sizes, colors and sartorial stripes pour out of classrooms, jostling and joking, filling the hallway with the buzz of pubescent energy. Then it's off to language arts, math, social studies and the array of other subjects offered at this sprawling arena for adolescents. A few blocks away, at Humboldt Park Elementary School, which serves kindergarten through eighth grade, a charming scene unfolds in Karen Hennessy's classroom. Her kindergartners are enjoying a visit from their eighth-grade "buddies." All around the room, big kids sit knees to chest in miniature chairs or cross-legged on the alphabet carpet. Each little kid has chosen a picture book to share with a big buddy. Some lean on eighth-grade laps as they listen. Logan Wells, a strapping 14-year-old, reads The Little Engine That Could to Alec Matias and Jacob Hill. Jacob, 5, seems mesmerized equally by the bright illustrations and by the eighth-grader turning the pages. He presses against Logan as if to absorb some *big-kid magic. The older boy reads on with gentle forbearance. If you were 13 years old, where would you rather be? Big, frenetic Fritsche, with its thrilling range of art classes, bands, Socratic seminars, and TV studio, all aimed at 1,030 sixth-, seventh- and eighth-graders? Or calm and cozy Humboldt Park, where the teachers seem to know the names and histories of all 585 students, ages 4 to 14? If you're the parent of a 13-year-old, which would you choose for your child? The two schools represent two sides of a debate that has ripped through Milwaukee and other U.S. cities. For the past decade, middle schools have been the educational setting for roughly two-thirds of students in Grades 6 through 8. But increasingly, communities are questioning whether they really are the best choice for this volatile age group.*

Some school districts have considered going back to the once traditional K-7, 8-12 grades model because of the many challenges and failings of the middle school concept. Why? Although 15 percent of schools in the Title I program (federal program to support low-income students) serve the middle grades, 33 percent of the schools in "Restructuring" or "Corrective Action" (measures of federally mandated intervention because the schools are not performing up to standards academically) are middle schools, according to the United States Government Accountability Office.

Middle schools are struggling so much that some members of Congress have suggested that something needs to be done to mend the middle schools. Perhaps students feel more comfortable and more confident in a K-7 school than in a school setting where the "Top Dogs" are eighth graders. Considering eighth graders as role models for sixth graders is a scary thought and is not conducive to a positive school climate.

Even if school districts wanted to eliminate middle schools it would be impossible to do now because the middle school concept is more than a concept; it is an institution and cottage industry that generates millions of dollars each year for textbook companies, test makers, software companies, consultants, and others. There are middle school conferences, middle school journals, middle school certification, college professors who specialize in middle school concepts, middle school awards, etc. Even though every public educator in America talks about "*data-driven decisions*," "best practices based on research," students are stuck with middle schools despite research that cites little support of the middle school concept.

In many communities across the country, more parents are looking for private schools during the middle school years for their children than for the high school years. In some states, public school enrollment drops in middle school and picks back up in high school. Yet, middle schools are so much a part of our culture, and not just an educational concept, that even if the data continued for years to show that middle schools are not effective and in fact play a major role in increasing the dropout rate, middle schools will remain. Some public education concepts become untouchable. Middle school is one of them.

For once in my life, my timing was good, because my school district at that time had not discovered the middle school concept. So, instead of contemplating dropping out when I was in the sixth grade, I delayed those thoughts until the eighth grade.

The year I entered high school is best remembered for the Civil Rights Act and the Economic Opportunity Act. Both acts changed the face and the dialogue of America. And public education continued to take a beating from writers and politicians. It was the beginning of the shift from respect for public schools to on-going political criticism of public education not from the perspective of trying to improve schools but from using public education to incite political advances of candidates and parties. University intellectuals realized they could cash in, also. Several professors who lacked any recognition because they wrote seldom read articles soon became best-selling authors and regulars on radio and television shows because they lambasted public education. Many of their epistles lacked evidence and too often their "solutions" were not grounded in logic or practicality.

An example, among many, was Paul Goodman's *Compulsory Mis-education,* which offered a wide-ranging critique of public education. He followed his criticism with the "cure" for public education. He had his own ideas of how to save or at least improve public education. He advocated provocative programs for improving education at the elementary, secondary and college level.

It is in the schools and from the mass media, rather than at home or from their friends, that the mass of our citizens in all classes learn that life is inevitably routine, depersonalized, venally graded; that it is best to toe the mark and shut up; that there is no place for spontaneity, open sexuality, free spirit. Trained in the schools, they go on to the same quality of jobs, culture, and politics. This

*is education, mis-education, socializing to the national
norms and regimenting to the national needs.*

Asserting that *"The compulsory system has become a
universal trap and it is no good,"* Goodman presented six
alternative proposals. The scary thing is that many people
took his proposals seriously and still do.

1. *Have 'no school at all' for a few classes. These
   children should be selected from tolerable, though
   not necessarily cultured homes. They should be
   neighbors and numerous enough to be a society for
   one another and so that they do not feel mere
   'different'. This experiment cannot do the children
   any academic harm since there is good evidence that
   normal children will make up the first seven years
   school-work with four to seven years of good
   teaching.* [This must be the most naïve and reckless
   recommendation in the annals of education fads. Not
   only is he advocating creating an elite class, he
   obviously knows very little about the teaching and
   learning process.]

2. *Dispense with the school building for a few classes;
   provide teachers and use the city itself as the school—
   its streets, cafeterias, stores, movies, museums,
   parks, and factories.* [This is a definition of field trips
   and learning journeys that teachers have used for
   decades.]

3. *Use appropriate unlicensed adults of the community
   —the druggist, the storekeeper, the mechanic—as the
   proper educators of the young into the grown-up
   world. Certainly, it would be a useful and animating*

experience for the adults. [What a radical idea to have various professionals come to the classrooms and talk about careers. I think it is called Career day. And I wonder if he's ever heard of apprenticeship programs?]

4. *Make class attendance not compulsory, in the manner of A.S. Neill's book,* Summerhill. *If the teachers are good, absence would tend to be eliminated; if they are bad, let them know it. The compulsory law is useful in getting the children away from their parents, but it must not result in trapping the children.* [At the same time, he was proposing this nonsense, states around the nation were recommending extending the compulsory attendance age to 18. Also, I'm sure every juvenile court judge in America would balk at his idea because they must deal with educational neglect daily.]

5. *Decentralize an urban school (or do not build a new big building) into small units, 20 to 50, in available storefronts or clubhouses. These tiny schools, equipped with record-player and pinball machines, could combine play, socializing, discussion, and formal teaching. For special events, the small units can be brought together into a common auditorium or gymnasium, to give the sense of the greater community.* [And will he provide the funding to build, staff, and operate these mini-play centers that do not seem focused on education?]

6. *Use a pro-rata part of the school money to send children to economically marginal farms for a couple of months a year, perhaps six children from mixed backgrounds to a farmer. The only*

requirement is that the farmer feeds them and not beat them; best, of course, if they take part in the farm work. [The "only" condition is that the children not be abused? There is no requirement that the farmers nurture them, encourage them, provide medical care, security, and other supportive living conditions – just don't abuse them. That's the only expectation.]

After only a week in high school, I was all for putting kids on the street for their education and I would have strongly supported his advice to let the adults of the community educate me instead of the teachers. Willie the Druggist, Clifford the Mechanic, Carmen the Beautician and John the Drug Dealer would have been more than glad to educate us high school students. Many of us skipped school in order to reach the level of education that Goodman advocated. We took to the streets and alleys for some of our education. And Goodman advocated pinball machines in schools.

Just when I thought the English teachers had rid the world of grammar because I was under the impression that the Grammar War was won by the good guys, my eighth grade English teacher announced on the very first day of school that *"You will master the eight parts of speech."* She should have added, *"Or throw up trying."* She said promotion to the ninth grade, getting a driver's license, having a girlfriend, and reaching adulthood depended on making a score of 100 on her eight parts of speech test. She did not get bogged down with all of that high-level curriculum theory stuff or how to write. She did not get hung up on pacing chapters so we would finish a certain chapter on the last day of school, as required by the state or local curriculum watchdog. None of that was relevant to her existence as an eighth grade English teacher and gatekeeper. She was the gatekeeper for high school. Fail her eight parts of speech tests enough times and you forfeited your high school career.

I do not remember how many times I took the eight parts of speech test; except I can still picture the seasons changing outside her classroom window during that eighth-grade year. However, I passed the test one day. Another student had something to do with it, but I will not go into details. Suffice to say, I did not cheat but without that student, I would still be in the eighth-grade class looking out the window. He taught me how to study methodically, and it worked.

The eighth grade offered many opportunities to observe weirdness. There was a peculiar looking guy in our eighth-grade classes at times who was introduced as something called a "Student Teacher." We were not sure what that meant or what he was supposed to do. A student teacher is not the same as a substitute teacher. They are a "wannabe" teacher. He certainly did not look like a student and he not look like a teacher either. I think that guy really was John Holt, whose book *How Children Fail* took the nation by storm because he could have used my eighth grade English classroom to illustrate and validate all his points.

Based on his observations in classrooms, Holt told real stories about teachers looking for "right answers," which does not seem so bad, but Holt argued that rote teaching and factual regurgitation suppressed abstraction, curiosity, appreciation, discovery, interaction, exploration, intrinsic motivation, and problem-solving, too.

In other words, forcing me to learn the eight parts of speech was stunting my intellectual growth and physical development though I might eventually get a driver's license I would not be an appreciative or courteous driver; and though I might have children someday, our only interaction would be about the eight parts of speech. I think Holt was on to something.

CHAPTER 8
THE LEVEL SYSTEM

If ignorance is bliss, why aren't there more happy people?

-Victor Cousins

Holt may have been in my English class at some time, but the influence of his book did not arrive fast enough. There was a student in my English class who made 100 on the first administration of the eight parts of speech test-a perfect score on the first try in early September in a Level 1 class (more on the Level system later) was remarkable. For the rest of the year, he read *Boy's Life* magazines.

One day he had the audacity to advise me on the best way to remember the bedeviled eight parts of speech. When the teacher spotted this un-American, subversive activity, he was banished from the room for two days. We never knew what happened to him during those two days and he refused to talk about it.

This same kid was a whiz at math and science and even history. He was one of the brightest kids I ever met in high school. He could talk about and do just about anything. He was the type of student who asked teachers questions that made them retreat to the textbooks for answers. His hair was almost always unkempt, and his clothes had that iron-like smell that comes from long-term neglect, but he could talk incessantly about anything and everything—class work, books, articles, weather, sports, life, religion, etc. I know he had to be bored in the remedial classes, and he was clearly a challeng to most of the teachers. He had the potential to go to college; however, he dropped out of school before the tenth grade due to boredom and a callous school climate.

Even though 1964 was a difficult year for public education, at least some were having great fun with (or at the expense of) public education. In a parody of public education, singer and songwriter Tom Paxton recorded the song *What Did You Learn in School Today?*

What did you learn in school today, dear little boy of mine?
I learned that Washington never told a lie.
I learned that soldiers seldom die.
I learned that everybody's free.
That is what the teacher said to me.
And that's what I learned in school today.
That's what I learned in school.

What did you learn in school today, dear little boy of mine?
I learned that policemen are my friends.
I learned that justice never ends.
I learned that murderers die for their crimes.
Even if we make a mistake sometimes.
And that's what I learned in school today.
That's what I learned in school.

What did you learn in school today, dear little boy of mine?
I learned that war is not so bad.
I learned about the great ones we have had.

We fought in Germany and France.
And someday I might get my chance.
And that's what I learned in school today.
That's what I learned in school.

What did you learn in school today, dear little boy of
mine?
I learned that our government must be strong.
It's always right and never wrong.
Our leaders are the finest men.
So we elect them again and again.
And that's what I learned in school today.
That's what I learned in school.

I would be remiss if I failed to mention two more important events when I entered high school: (1) my introduction to public education's "Level System" and (2) the publication of Gary Becker's legendary book, *Human Capital*.

In elementary school, I certainly did not distinguish myself as a budding scholar, but I was not the worse student in my classes either. I seldom missed a day of school, only got in a few fights, seldom talked back to a teacher, seldom missed turning in homework and projects on time although the quality ebbed and flowed, did not bring dishonor to the school, did not use profanity, and was on the safety patrol (for a short period of time). Nevertheless, I learned in October of my eighth-grade year and first year in high school that I had been placed in something called "Level 1" classes. I thought that must be a good thing until my intelligent soon-to-be dropout classmate explained to me that Level 1 was at the bottom of the public education pecking order, two social strata below the elegance of Level 3 designation.

My friend also explained that no student had ever risen above Level 1. Once a student is labeled Level 1, that student remains a member of the Level 1 proletariat for life. I was upset. I told my parents and they did not seem too concerned about it. They just wanted me to get a high school diploma and said I should suck it up, tough it out and do what the teachers said to do. After all, their perspective was shaped by the lack of education; neither one made it to high school.

I was in the eighth grade and I simply didn't care anymore–the minimal effort was the method and expectation, which was reinforced by the minimal effort of teachers. Believe me, the teachers of Level 1 students were not reading Carl Sandburg to the classes.

Aside from my bitter disappointment and "placement", I wondered how talented students could be in Level 1, also. The student I mentioned earlier was a renaissance kid; he knew a lot about everything. How could he be in Level 1? If it was a simple bureaucratic error for me to be in Level 1, it must have been a case of mistaken identity for him to be in Level 1. I began to understand later why he dropped out of school. I also later determined that the reason he was in Level 1 probably had something to do with his appearance and socioeconomic status – he was clearly a poor kid who probably had one meal a day, the school lunch. I don't recall seeing any students in Level 3 (the top echelon) that looked like or dressed like that kid or me. It appeared that socioeconomic status was a determining factor for level placements. A total disservice to all children.

The Level System was not much different than the classification of students that Ray Rist wrote about in an article for the Harvard Review entitled *The Self-Fulfilling Prophecy*, based on the work of the sociologist Robert Merton (*Social Theory and Social Structure*).

Rist found that numerous students were grouped according to their social status: the middle-class students were the "Tigers;" the students from working-class families were the "Cardinals;" and the poor students carried the name, "Clowns." The Level System in my school district as in many school districts across America at that time closely paralleled the social status system that Rist refers to in his article.

I never considered my family as poor. My parents worked long hours and we lived in a small house. We seldom took a vacation. However, we had food on the table; we had clothes; we had a car (I guess you could call a used Packard a car), and we enjoyed each other as a family. We had difficult times, like when my parents lost their little dairy farm and later when my father lost his job, but we endured. We were not a complaining family, and my mother was at her best when times were toughest. In all of the ways that matter, we were not poor.

As I would find out during my experiences with public education, where a student is placed in class to a large extent determines his future because it is directly related to the quality of education he will receive much like predicted in Robert Rosenthal's book *Pygmalion in the Classroom*.

In a classic study conducted by Rosenthal and Jacobson, they told teachers in a public school they identified 20 students in 18 classrooms that were "academic spurters," even though the students were randomly selected. Sure enough, those intellectual spurters bloomed, because that was what the teachers expected. Imagine the expectations of teachers teaching Level 1 students compared to the expectation of teachers teaching Level 2 and 3 students. What type of classroom climate do they create?

While public schools slowly moved away from the overt classification of students, similar types of classifications and corresponding expectations takes place in today's public schools. Just look at the percentage of students in low income, rural, or urban schools who do not have access to Advanced Placement classes (more challenging classes with some of the best teachers).

According to a study conducted by the United States Department of Education, over 40 percent of high schools in America do not offer any Advanced Placement courses. And guess which socio-economic group is overrepresented in the 40 percent? Poor kids. Why is access to Advanced Placement classes important?

If anyone can think of an academic program in the last decade that has had as positive an impact on American public high schools as Advanced Placement, I would like to hear what it is. I can't think of any that comes even close." (Jay Mathews). Mathews is the author of *Class Struggle: What is wrong (and Right) About America's Best Public High Schools.*

He points out by example that students from all social status groups can enhance their chances of attending and succeeding in college if they are exposed to Advanced

Placement classes in high school; yet, public education provides that opportunity to a low percentage of public high school students. In other words, all the "Eagles" and some of the "Tigers" have that chance, but the "Clowns" do not. Add rural school students to the latter group because they do not have access to AP classes either.

It represents the power of expectations and the inequity of opportunity. It represents the opportunities in public education, the opportunities that Malcolm Gladwell so poignantly showed in his book *Outliers* that are essential for success–a chance at a good education. As Gladwell writes, just give all kids an equal chance.

As I moved from classroom to classroom and to other places in my high school such as the cafeteria, hallways, library, counseling office, and as I observed and interacted with other eighth grade students, it became obvious that there was a "place" for Level 1 kids and a very different "place" for Level 2 and Level 3 kids. I am sure it was mere coincidence that the Level 3 kids dressed better than the Level 2 and Level 1 kids. And I know it was only by chance that most of the athletic type kids landed in either Level 2 or Level 3.

Think of the other advantages. The best teachers worked with Level 3 students and created positive classroom climates. The most vocal parents would support the school and the larger good of public education. Level 2 kids and parents were the salt of the earth–middle class, the teacher-and-principal-are-always-right type of parents, the social climbers. This is where young teachers with potential were placed. At Level 2, the principal and the Level 3 teachers could pass judgment on whether a young Level 2 teacher deserved working with Level 3 students in the future, or if they needed more years learning and perfecting their craft at Level 2. Level 3 teachers knew the importance of a positive school climate.

Later in my life when I started my professional education career in the same school district where I had earlier been labeled Level 1, I was told that the Level System benefitted students because they could work at their ability level. Besides, I was told, the students do not pay any attention to what Level they are in and most do not even know what Level they are in. That is a myth. Did educators really believe that? Every student knew the Level of every other student in the entire high school and Level 1 students were reminded of their lowly status almost every day by Level 2 and Level 3 students and teachers.

Why do I include my experience with the notorious Level System in the same breath with Gary Becker's book, *Human Capital*? First, let me tell you about the impact of Becker's book. Becker, who would be awarded the Nobel Prize in Economics, pointed out as early as 1964 that a good education is a key to the financial survival of a nation. He was not talking about a good education for certain students; he was talking about a good education for *all* students. His book became a standard reference for many years in economic circles, but it should have been and even today should be required reading for all educators, businessmen, parents, supporters, and critics of public education. It remains timely, relevant, and poignant.

According to Becker, financial capital cannot develop or even exist without "human capital." Human capital is the education and training that focuses on human development, for only through that approach will human potential be realized, according to Becker. Therefore, funding for education and efforts to educate all citizens are an investment in human capital and ultimately the financial stability for the nation. While people can be separated from their financial and physical assets, Becker says, people cannot be separated from their knowledge, skills, health, or values. Think about the students driven out of high school or middle school and the subsequent lost wages. It's a quality of life issue with serious economic development consequences, too.

Becker was one of the first to see that education is the most important investment in human capital. Becker found many studies showings a high school and college education in the United States greatly raise a person's income, even after netting out direct and indirect costs of schooling, and even after adjusting for family income levels.

Public education represents a major portion of each state's budget and the federal government pumps billions of dollars into public education, but it is not enough. Public education has never been fully funded in the United States in a way that focuses on the relationship between access, equity, quality, and the conditions and needs of students. Many politicians claim that public education receives too much money now and that there is no correlation between money and student achievement. However, not everyone agrees with that. Funding for public education is not an expense; it is an investment.

The state of Maryland saw what Becker saw and dedicated two billion dollars to improve education. What were the results? Read what was reported in the Baltimore Sun Times:

Five years after Maryland increased spending by $2 billion to provide greater academic equity, students have made remarkable gains in reading and math, according to a report given to the Maryland General Assembly by an outside consultant. For every additional $1,000 spent per student, there was a significant increase in pass rates in both subjects. The improvement was twice as great for middle school students as for those in elementary grades." The report by MGT of America also confirms what most educators have intuitively believed for decades: Money invested in teachers appears to pay off. About 80 percent of additional local and state funding has been spent on the teaching staff - raising salaries, hiring more to reduce class sizes and requiring a highly qualified teacher in every classroom.

Notice the emphasis on the quality of the teachers and the relationship between teacher quality and student achievement. School climate also improved, which allowed more productive learning climates to emerge that fostered student connectedness and engagement.

Another example comes from Georgia, where then-governor Sonny Perdue invested millions of dollars in "graduation coaches" to increase the graduation rate. The state's graduation rate increased every year after that, right up to the point he stopped the funding for graduation coaches and balanced the state's budget deficit at the expense of public education (with a one-billion-dollar reduction) during the Great Recession. The graduation coach concept was effective because it focused on developing relationships and engaging students in school. It enhanced social-emotional engagement. The graduation coaches became mentors for the students, so the students felt more connected to the school. Those are elements of a positive school climate.

Becker said a nation's survival depends on education. He was right.

So, what would Becker think of the Level System? Becker made the first connection between education as a means of national survival, not based on some abstract notions of an intellectual, but instead on the direct link between educating everyone and economic development and national survival. This connection strongly suggests that dehumanizing concepts such as the Level System and other forms of segregation are not only unholy and inhuman but downright dangerous for a nation.

As mentioned earlier, if public education has the research that shows students who take Advanced Placement exams are better prepared for college than those that do not and consequently are less likely to drop out, then why is an economically disadvantaged student, or a rural student, or an urban student less likely than a student from a middle class or upper class family to attend a school that does not offer many if any Advanced Placement classes?

Georgia made a concentrated effort to increase and widen access to Advanced Placement classes – even adding on-line classes. At the same time it focused on improving school climate. Georgia's graduation rate increased from 67 percent to 82 percent.

CHAPTER 9
BLOOM OR BUST

Education is learning what you didn't even know you didn't know.

–Daniel Boorstin

The Elementary and Secondary Education Act (ESEA), designed by Commissioner of Education Francis Keppel, was passed on April 9, 1965, less than three months after it was introduced, and just a few months before I finally passed the damn eight parts of speech test in the never-ending eighth grade English class.

ESEA provided funding for public education with considerable funding for low-income students, even though most of the funding for public education came from, and still does, states and local school districts.

ESEA was part of an important educational component of the "War on Poverty" launched by President Lyndon B. Johnson. Through special funding (Title I), it allocated resources to meet the needs of "educationally deprived children," especially through compensatory programs for the poor. ESEA stated:

In recognition of the special educational needs of low-income families and the impact that concentrations of low-income families have on the ability of local educational agencies to support adequate educational programs, the Congress hereby declares it to be the policy of the United States to provide financial assistance... to local educational agencies serving areas with concentrations of children from low-income families to expand and improve their educational programs by various means (including preschool programs) which contribute to meeting the special educational needs of educationally deprived children.

This was the beginning of *Head Start* (Head Start is a preschool program for disadvantaged children aiming at equalizing equality of opportunity based on 'readiness' for the first grade that was originally started by the Office of Economic Opportunity as an eight-week summer program, and quickly expanded to a full-year program.) *Follow-Through* (to complement the gains made by children who participated in the Head Start Program), *Bilingual Education* (targeting mainly Spanish-speaking children), and a variety of guidance and counseling programs followed. This was a noble effort in the United States to address issues of access and equity in public education, but both continued to be a problem and challenge.

While I struggled with the mind-numbing experience of the ninth grade, and while the nation was trying to address some of the problems of public education, "Bloom's Taxonomy" burst on the education scene with support from the writers of ESEA.

Bloom's Taxonomy was originally created in and for an academic context when Benjamin Bloom chaired a committee of educational psychologists whose aim was to develop a system of categories of learning behavior to assist in the design and assessment of educational learning and curriculum design.

Bloom believed that education should focus on "mastery" of subjects and the promotion of higher forms of thinking, rather than a utilitarian approach to simply memorize and transfer facts and figures. Rote memorization was the most rewarded type of intelligence in public schools. Typically, creativity was not recognized, endorsed or rewarded. A kid who could memorize a textbook was destined to become a doctor, while a kid who sat in the corner of the classroom writing poetry or a short story, was at best destined to be a Level 1 teacher.

Bloom demonstrated that most teachers focused on fact-transfer and information recall, which is the lowest level of teaching. Rote learning was pervasive across all levels of learning, according to Bloom. That is one reason why so much emphasis was placed on IQ scores and pure memorization.

Bloom's Taxonomy model is in three parts, or "overlapping domains".

1. *Cognitive domain (intellectual capability, i.e., knowledge, or 'think')*
2. *Affective domain (feelings, emotions and behavior, i.e., attitude, or 'feel')*
3. *Psychomotor domain (manual and physical skills, i.e., skills, or 'do')*

Colleges and universities around the nation immediately identified Bloom's Taxonomy as the new framework for teaching, learning, and training. Even the business world latched on to Bloom's Taxonomy and applied the concepts to corporate training programs. It is difficult to understand now how radical and enlightening Bloom's concepts were at that time to public education.

Bloom not only advocated the alteration of teaching and learning, but he also made teaching more complicated, more relevant, more productive, more engaging, and more professional. In addition to skills, teachers were expected to teach students how to think, how to make connections, how to use logic coupled with an understanding of the affective domain. While Bloom never explicitly referenced school and classroom climate, he highlighted the essential components of engagement and connectedness, which are strong classroom and school climate elements.

Colleges and universities altered their teacher training programs to be more aligned with Bloom's Taxonomy. However, the "Bloomers," like some newly minted and enthusiastic teachers where called by the veteran teachers, were discouraged from using this newfangled teaching style and view of teaching. This disconnect created a wide gulf between college and university teacher preparation programs and teaching in the real world of public education. Many universities did not prepare teachers for the public education world, nor did they teach the teachers how to incorporate Bloom's taxonomy into an existing framework in schools. The educational enlightenment of Bloom's work traveled very slowly to public education in the South.

The fact-transfer and information recall that Bloom loathed was in full bloom in my high school. There really was not much fact-transfer and only marginal information recall, because those *were* higher forms of thinking for my classmates. The primary expectation was to say "yes, mam" to the teacher, avoid the parts of the high school frequented by the sadistic bullies, and resist eating or sniffing the chalk dust. Anything rising above those behaviors and expectations was asking too much.

A most memorable event brightened my high school career when one of my teachers displayed both a concern for his students and a sense of humor. I am not sure which was the most surprising. I had not laughed or even smiled in a classroom in a long time. The class was of all things Earth Science. Earth Science was offered to students who still thought the earth was flat and could not spell "Science."

The Earth Science teacher learned our names. We were used to the method that cut down the confusion prevalent in most of my classes where the teachers would yell, "*Hey, you!*" to students. Suddenly and quite unexpectedly we were not a classroom filled with a bunch of no-names. The teacher greeted us at the door, used our names, and told at least one joke each day. He nurtured a positive classroom climate.

One time he told us he was two and a half billion years old because in his youth the age of the Earth was known to be two billion years old and now it is known to be 4.5 billion years. We did not always understand his jokes, but we laughed anyway because he was interested in us, interesting when he taught, and he had a great attitude. He did not fit the norm at all. Maybe he knew about Bloom's Affective Domain. Maybe Bloom's work reached a few teachers at the school level in the Deep South, or maybe he was naturally a caring teacher who wanted to make a difference in the lives of children.

CHAPTER 10
WHEN TRAVESTY BECOMES TRAGEDY

In our infinite ignorance, we are all equal.
-Karl Popper

In the 1960s being with each other was a challenging concept. There was a great deal of unrest across the nation, primarily because of growing race relations issues.

A study commissioned by the U.S. Office of Education in accordance with the Civil Rights Act, what was to be known as the *Coleman Report*, named after the principal researcher, James S. Coleman, and turned public education and politics upside down. The issues of racial relations, equality, and access were foremost in the public's consciousness, and Coleman's study added fuel to the fire. The *Coleman Report* is widely considered one of the most important public education studies of the 20th century.

Using data from over 600,000 students and teachers across the country, the researchers found that academic achievement was less related to the quality of a student's school and more related to the social composition of the school, the student's sense of control of his environment (school climate) and his future, the verbal skills of teachers, and a student's family background. I could have saved Coleman a lot of time and money if he only interviewed me because I could have told him all the above are related to school climate.

My attitude toward race relations started early in my life with my parents. They may have been uneducated in the traditional sense, but they were Phi Beta Kappa in life, attitude, honesty, integrity, and fair play.

One particularly compelling point in my budding attitude toward minorities occurred in a hay field near my home in Stone Mountain, Georgia. Yes, Stone Mountain, Georgia, known for years as a Klu Klux Klan stronghold. Stone Mountain, a huge granite mountain that at the time was private property, is where the KKK proudly displayed burning crosses. Near the tiny town of Stone Mountain, at the base of the mountain and in nearby corn and hay fields, the KKK often held rallies, even into the late 1950s and early 1960s. The site of these rallies was a short distance from my childhood home.

My father was a hard-working man with a sense of humanity and decency that was rare in that area of Georgia. He came from a dirt-poor family that scratched out a living in rural Georgia as best it could on a tenant farm. He was also a veteran of World War II, having served in the Pacific Theatre during the height of the action. My father was a Navy Seabee, the construction wing of the Navy.

Shortly after Pearl Harbor, the Navy realized the need for a militarized Naval Construction Force to build advance airbases in war zones. The first recruits were the men who had built the Boulder Dam, the national highways, New York's skyscrapers, local buildings, schools, and houses; who had worked in the mines and quarries and dug the subway tunnels; who had worked in shipyards and built docks and wharfs and even ocean liners and aircraft carriers. By the end of the war, 325,000 such men served in the Seabees. They knew more than 60 skilled trades, but as a Seabee, they were also expected to fight when necessary.

Typically, the Seabees came ashore an atoll as soon as the Marines secured the beaches and started moving inland. The Seabees built airstrips as fast as possible so planes with supplies could land. This was part of the island-hopping strategy in the Pacific. It is not commonly known that the Seabees played a major role in the Atlantic Theatre as well. There is a statue of a Seabee at the entrance to Arlington National Cemetery. While in the Seabees, my father made several friends and race did not matter in a war zone. He brought many of those interracial friendships home after the war.

When I was very young, about 9 or 10 years old, my father told me one afternoon to get in his truck and ride with him. We rambled down a dirt road in an old dairy truck that during the day was used to deliver milk to both white and black families. A tree-lined dirt road turned into an open field filled with hundreds of people wearing white sheets over their heads and bodies. The white sheets billowed in the wind. They were standing around burning crosses and shouting epitaphs. I had heard of such events. After all, Stone Mountain was for decades a haven for the KKK. In fact, Samuel Hoyt Venable was a grandmaster in the KKK and owned Stone Mountain. He allowed the KKK to have meetings at the mountain and in nearby fields long before the State of Georgia took control of Stone Mountain.

I was puzzled by this impromptu trip. My father was a purposeful man, who did not waste time, but on that afternoon his purpose was not clear, and he was unusually quiet. His purpose for driving to the KKK rally was soon very clear. When he stopped the truck on the side of the road across the railroad tracks from the KKK rally he said

Garry, I want you to see this. At some time in your life you are going to have to decide whether you are a racist or not, and if you're going to let others lead you into what they do even though you know it's wrong, it's something you'll have to live with.

That is all he said. I did not say a word; I did not know what to say or ask. I was not sure what it all meant at that time, but he wanted to plant that seed. We sat there for a few minutes longer and then he drove us back home in silence. That was the awakening to my choices and the influences of others. It was one of my father's many ways of telling me about people.

My adventures in high school continued. Most of the day was one dull movement from classroom to classroom. The highlight of the day was P.E. and lunch. The P.E. teacher was also the head football coach who had a great attitude and who enjoyed playing with the students in all P.E. activities. No tetherball with him.

My tenth-grade History teacher was a bully. He was loud, obnoxious and thought teaching a class with a paddle of wood in his hands was proof of his superiority and authority. He walked around the class with a paddle in his hand. He thought it was clever or macho to periodically, for no apparent reason, slam the wooden paddle down on a student's wooden desk so hard that it sounded like a rifle shot. The teacher intentionally intimidated and picked on everyone in the class, but the target of most of his bully tactics was a quiet kid who was seldom alert and even less interested in school. One day the teacher harassed the student unmercifully one too many times. The student never said a word nor did he even look at the teacher. When the teacher yelled across the room that the student's family was *"probably all stupid like you"* I had the same sensation you get when you hear a strange noise in the dark of night – dread and fear. The student slowly looked up at the teacher but did not say a word. The teacher, not knowing well enough to leave him alone, rushed toward him and challenged him yelling, *"Why are you looking at me, boy?"* As the student stood up to leave the classroom, the teacher hit him across the back of his shoulder with the paddle, shouting for the student to sit down. The student turned around, grabbed the paddle from the teacher's hand and threw it down with a vengeance. He then just stood there staring at the teacher. We knew he was trying to control his anger, which is a good thing for the teacher because the student would have killed him. We were all pulling for the student to kill him. Why he did not clobber the teacher we will never know, because we never saw the student again. We never heard anything about him and no one knew him well enough to find out what happened to him. Not too long after this cruel episode with teacher and student, the teacher found all four of his tires flat when he left school one day. The student had friends. We were his friends. Perhaps we should have told him we were his friends.

Today, many people complain about the laws and regulations that protect students. I don't complain, because I remember vulnerable kids who should have been protected and nurtured and encouraged by people but who instead were ostracized, ridiculed, and tossed away.

On a whim one year, I tried out for the varsity baseball team. Considering my low-profile view of life and my low level of self-expectations, this was a major risk for me. I was a good athlete and played recreation league baseball with some success during the long, hot summer months. I had always loved baseball. I would catch the afternoon newspaper that was delivered by the same minister with the fallout shelter. I could forgive his attitude about nuclear war, God, and his own survival because each day he delivered the baseball scores via a newspaper. With the smell of newspaper print ink in the air, I read the Sports page on the floor. I poured through the baseball box scores. I propped my chin on my hands with my elbows carefully spread across the page as the details in the box scores helped recreate the games in my mind.

To my surprise, I made the varsity baseball team, but shortly thereafter the fatherly and dedicated baseball coach left the school to attend to his gravely ill father living in another state. The coach was replaced with the football team's line coach. I guess the goon was the only coach who showed any interest in getting the small salary supplement that came with the job. He was large, obnoxious, loud, aggressive, and unpredictable – all the essential qualities of a football line coach. However, he did not know anything about baseball. He was so abrasive and outrageous that some of the players quit. Then one day after practice he lost control. He screamed at all of us because he didn't think we were running the bases fast enough. He yelled for us to gather together in a group on the pitcher's mound. As we all stood there, he started berating us, yelling and screaming at the top of his lungs with profanity pouring forth through his spit. He was stomping around with a baseball bat in his hand pounding the ground with it while he called us worthless creatures. Suddenly, he stopped and without warning threw the bat at us as hard as he could. Most of us saw the bat coming at us like a loose saw blade and ducked out of the way, but one poor kid standing in the middle of the group did not see the bat and therefore did not move. The hard-flung bat hit him square in his chest. The collision made the sound like dropping a watermelon; everyone could hear all of the air leaving his lungs. He dropped to his knees clutching his chest and toppled over on his face. I thought he was dead. We all did. As a group, we all rushed over to him and found him gasping for air. A teacher witnessed the episode, called 911, and rushed to the player. The player continued to gasp for air until the paramedics arrived and gave him oxygen. The player stayed overnight in the hospital with broken ribs.

What a great role model the baseball coach and P.E. teacher turned out to be. Most of the players left the team. I would have left the team, also, but I loved baseball too much to quit.

The goon continued to coach and teach at the same high school until spring football training one year when he made a small football player run the ball between two very large tacklers. Without anyone to block for him, they, of course, clobbered him. The coach saw some perverse humor in this and made the poor kid run the same drill two more times. One of the larger players told the coach that the smaller player was going to get hurt. He was cursed and told to keep tackling. As the players feared, the small player did not get up after being tackled hard for at least the fifth or sixth time. Several players rushed to him, but the coach pushed them out of the way and jerked the kid up off the ground, called him a few profane names, and sent him to the locker room. No one went with the player as he stumbled across the practice field. After practice, over an hour later, they found the injured player unconscious in the locker room. He later died in a hospital. Finally, the coach left.

CHAPTER 11
EXPECTATIONS COME AND GO

One isn't born one's self. One is born with a mass of expectations, a mass of other people's ideas, and you must work through it all.

– V.S. Naipaul

A lot has been written about expectations, the power of expectations, the nature of expectations, the outcome of expectations, and the promise of expectations.

To some people, certain students are not expected to do well so they don't do well but sometimes they were not given the chance to do well. Too many students with special needs, minority students, and low-income students suffer at the hands of people who do not think the students are capable of learning.

It is important to note that the concept and importance of high and low expectations that many public educators dismiss as an intrusion into education had cause to rethink their attitudes when the book *Pygmalion in the Classroom* was published and republished and validated in numerous replication studies since the original work. I earlier referenced the work of Rosenthal and Jacobson, but it's important to know more specific information about their work.

In what has become a classic in the sociology of education and human nature, researchers Rosenthal and Jacobson's experiment took place in a public elementary school in a predominantly low socio-economic community. At the beginning of the school year, the researchers gave students an intelligence test they called "The Harvard Test of Inflected Acquisition." They told the teachers that not only did this test determine intelligence quotients (IQs), but it could also identify those students who could make rapid, above-average intellectual progress in the coming year.

Before the next school year began, teachers received the names of those students who, based on the test, could be expected to perform well. However, Rosenthal and Jacobson had randomly picked these names from the class list. The test did not identify "academic spurters" as the teachers had been led to believe. Any differences between these children and the rest of the class existed only in the minds of the teachers. A second intelligence test was administered at the end of the school year. Those students who had been identified as "academic spurters" showed, on average, an increase of more than 12 points on their IQ scores, compared to an increase of 8 points among the rest of the students. The differences were even larger in the early grades, with almost half of first- and second-grade "spurters" showing an IQ increase of 20 points or more.

Teachers' subjective assessments, such as reading grades, showed similar differences. The teachers also indicated that these "special" students were better behaved, were more intellectually curious, had greater chances for future success, and were friendlier than their counterparts. Rosenthal and Jacobson concluded that a "self-fulfilling prophecy" was at work. The teachers had subtly and unconsciously encouraged and rewarded the performance they expected to see and created conditions in the classroom that promoted and encouraged students. The teachers improved their classroom climates. Not only did they spend more time with these students, but they were also more enthusiastic about teaching them and showed more warmth and concern for them than the other students. As a result, the academic spurters felt more capable, more engaged and intelligent, and they performed accordingly – they lived up to the expectations of the teachers.

Interestingly, over 350 studies have since validated Rosenthal and Jacobson's conclusions. Included in these studies are various biases of expectations, such as:

1. *Gender- lower expectations are often held for older girls, particularly in scientific and technical areas, because of gender-role stereotyping.*
2. *Socio-Economic Status- teachers sometimes hold lower expectations of students from low socio-economic backgrounds.*
3. *Race/Ethnicity- students from minority races or ethnic groups are sometimes viewed as less capable than other students.*
4. *Type of School- students from urban schools and rural schools are sometimes presumed to be less capable than students from suburban schools.*
5. *Appearance- the value or style of students' clothes and students' grooming habits can influence teachers' expectations.*
6. *Oral Language Patterns- the presence of any nonstandard English- speaking pattern can sometimes lead teachers to hold lower expectations.*
7. *Messiness/ Disorganization- students whose work areas or assignments are messy are sometimes perceived as having a lower ability.*

8. *Readiness- immaturity or lack of experience may be confused with learning ability leading to low expectations.*

9. *Halo Effect- some teachers generalize from one characteristic a student may have, thereby making unfounded assumptions about the student's overall ability or behavior.*

10. *Seating Position- if students seat themselves at the sides or back of the classroom some teachers perceive this as a sign of lower learning motivation and/or ability and treat students accordingly.*

11. *Negative Comments about Students- teachers' expectations are sometimes influenced by the negative comments of other staff members about students.*

12. *Outdated Theories- educational theories which stress the limitations of learners can lead to lowered expectations.*

13. *Tracking or Long-Term Ability Groups- placement in "low" tracks or groups can cause students to be viewed as having less learning potential than they actually have.*

Rosenthal and Jacobson's book ends with a quote from George Bernard Shaw's play "Pygmalion":

You see, really and truly, apart from the things anyone can pick up (the dressing and the proper way of speaking, and so on), the difference between a lady and a flower girl is not how she behaves, but how she's treated. I shall always be a flower girl to Professor Higgins, because he always treats me as a flower girl,

and always will; but I know I can be a lady to you,
because you always treat me like a lady, and always will.

I know Pygmalion lived in my high school: Level 1, Level 2 and Level 3. The monster of biased expectation was not born in my high school, but it was reproduced and nurtured every year. Some Level 2 and Level 3 kids did not live up to expectations, but almost all Level 1 kids lived down to expectations. In addition to low academic expectations, we were expected to misbehave and drift toward delinquent behavior and later in life become a low-wage earner. Far too many lived up (or down) to that expected future in many ways.

In his terrific book, *Raising the Grade*, the former Governor of West Virginia, Bob Wise, wrote:

Despite the oft-stated claim that every child has an equal opportunity to reach for the stars academically, and that the once widely-used 'tracking' of students has been abandoned, there are clear differences in classroom preparedness and resources for various subgroups. These differences often translate into negative effects on academic achievement, graduation rate, and college attendance and graduation. Even as kids in my hometown, forty years later, still refer to themselves as hill kids or creekers, the reality is that race and class issues continue to play a role in influencing the quality of education students receive nationwide.

I did a lot of things that were troubling and downright dangerous, but drugs were not one of them. Alcohol, yes, but no drugs such as LSD, marijuana, or

Heroin. A classmate of mine nicknamed "Speed" (and not because he drove a car fast) was the type of high school kid who had a beard when he was in the ninth grade and was talking about sex and drugs even earlier. Speed had already started drifting away from high school, but when a teacher told him to get a haircut it only hastened Speed's disinterest in school.

There was more to it than that. Speed told that teacher to stick it up his ass. After Speed made his comment, the teacher walked slowly around the room and a few minutes later, very deliberately grabbed Speed's long hair and pulled on it. Before we could catch a breath, Speed had the teacher by the collar and was punching him repeatedly in the stomach. Some students pulled Speed away from the teacher, but by then the teacher was doubled over and throwing up. Speed ran out of the classroom. The teacher shrugged off another teacher's offer of help and sat down at his desk. When he composed himself, the teacher never said a word. A few minutes later, the principal brought Speed to the classroom and demanded to know what happened. To my knowledge, neither the teacher nor Speed and certainly no one in the classroom, ever revealed what happened.

That afternoon, Speed asked me for a ride home. I did not consider Speed a friend, simply because I did not know him except in a couple of classes. Nevertheless, I took him home on the way to my part-time job at a gas station. Speed promptly lit up a marijuana joint in my car, just as easily as the rest of us lit up a cigarette. With his long hair flowing in the breeze of an open window of my car, he was as laid back as a person could be considering that he had just earlier that day been in a fight with a teacher. He never said a word about the incident while we were in the car.

When we reached Speed's modest home, I saw an old car in the driveway. It was a beat up 1959 Ford that Speed drove to school when it was operational. He told me he would pay me ten dollars to take him to downtown Atlanta later that night, plus he would fill my gas tank. The ten dollars was a lot of money at that time, but the offer to fill up my gas-guzzling car ensured his ride to Atlanta. Also, he asked me if he could ride with me to school until he repaired his car. I am not sure why he asked me to give him a ride to Atlanta and to school, but it didn't appear that Speed had very many friends.

When I returned that evening to Speed's home, we moved some stuff from his car to my car. I was shocked to find what was in his car. I was not surprised to see some marijuana joints at various stages of use, but I was surprised to see so many books in his car. He had his textbooks, which was a modest surprise, but he also had novels, poetry books, a pictorial book about National Parks, several National Geographic Magazines, Mad Magazine, Life Magazine, a tattered copy of a Reader's Digest Condensed Books and a local newspaper. I naturally thought they all belonged to his mom, but when I scooped some of them up and headed toward his house, he told me those were his. He said he loved to read and write.

As we drove to Atlanta, I heard about some of the demons in Speed's head and life – an abusive and now absent father, a hard-working and depressed single-parent mom, a kid bored out of his mind at school, the dark side of depression, and a very lonely kid.

When we arrived on Peachtree Street in downtown Atlanta that night, Speed gave me directions to 14th Street. In the 1960s suburban families found recreation in driving through Atlanta to see and jeer at the "hippies" who settled between 10th and 14th streets, on sidewalks and in the alleyways. It was a show for those born and raised in the conservative south to see hippies in all form of dress doing all types of things right there in downtown Atlanta. Families would drive to the legendary downtown "Varsity," the mainstay hot dog and hamburger joint, and then after a good greasy meal hop back in the car and drive to the freak show on 14th street. It was the perfect family outing. It was also good fodder for every preacher within 100 miles of Atlanta who needed an example of Godlessness in American society.

I parked the car and as we walked into the alleys between the streets called the "Catacombs," Speed told me to stay close to him and to keep my mouth shut. The atmosphere changed from one of love and dove to dark and sinister. Drug dealing and using were taking place in the open.

Speed stopped at a doorway covered with the glossy painting of a red dragon. He knocked on the door as he looked nervously all around. The door opened quickly, and Speed was ushered in, but when I took a step to follow him I was abruptly and forcefully pushed back toward the alley. As I moved back toward the door, a handgun appeared in the hand of a nasty-looking character. Speed stepped between us and told me to wait outside. I waited in the alley for Speed with a realization that Speed lived in a world far different from mine and most others. This was my first glimpse at the underbelly of the illegal drug world and addiction.

When Speed appeared in the doorway about 30 minutes after entering the Dragon's den, it was obvious he was not the same person. By the time we reached Speed's house that night, he was so high I had to carry him to his room. When we entered his house, his mother didn't say a word. She just looked away.

A few weeks later, he and his mother moved away. I heard two years later that Speed died from an overdose. I was not surprised but I was truly saddened by the news. Speed had personal demons, of course, but Speed also had an active and inquisitive mind, the kind of mind that teachers with high expectations can nurture and develop.

The power of expectations cannot be overstated.

CHAPTER 12
LEARNING CONDITIONS

Bad things are not the worst things that can happen to us.

−Richard Bach

It is difficult for any person who did not live through the assassination of John F. Kennedy to understand even remotely how the events impacted our world and our psyche and our attitude toward life and the future. To many children, the assassination of President Kennedy took away their sense of innocence and security. Those same children just a few years later had to live through and try to find some meaning in the assassinations of Martin Luther King, Jr. and Robert Kennedy in the same year. This was also a time of civil disobedience and debate over the Viet Nam War.

Generations did not trust each other. Many members of the Greatest Generation were parents of teenagers and young adults struggling through the emotional cauldron of the era. They could not understand how anyone could question the United States' presence, purpose, or motivation in Viet Nam. The Greatest Generation was concerned about the notion of something called "limited engagement" in Viet Nam. It brought back bad memories of Korea where similar terms were used. To them, it was either war or not. However, they were reluctant to criticize the United States government and would never question the military. That generation also struggled to understand hippies and war protesters.

Many parents of one generation supported the war effort in Viet Nam while so many of the next generation criticized the war. A lot of young people were caught in between.

Many of us were still influenced by our parents, and thus thought we should support the war effort. This attitude was reflected in my high school. There was an "Affirmation Viet Nam" Rally in the Fulton County Stadium, the stadium for professional baseball and football in Atlanta at that time. I am not sure why my high school participated in the Affirmation Viet Nam Rally, because many of the attendees were college students.

A couple of Emory University (Atlanta, Georgia) students decided they were tired of the war protests and made plans to develop a pro-Viet Nam rally. College and some high school students from all over the Atlanta area and beyond attended the rally on a rainy day in 1966. At my high school, we were packed into school buses and transported to the stadium whether we supported the Viet Nam war or not. The stadium at that time held over 50,000 people. *Time* magazine later reported that over 10,000 students attended the rally. The keynote speaker was then Secretary of State Dean Rusk. There were reports that singer Anita Bryant was going to attend, but she was too sick to make an appearance. The most compelling moment of the entire rally was the performance by Sgt. Barry Sadler, a Green Beret, who sang his hit song "The Green Beret," which was later featured in a John Wayne movie by the same name. Sgt. Sadler was a striking figure in his Army uniform with his Green Beret and an impressive number of medals on his chest. Armed with only a guitar, his voice rang strong and true throughout the stadium. After his performance, no one complained any more about the rain.

After the rally, we were brought back to school. It was clear in my high school that "we" supported the Viet Nam war. I had very mixed feelings because my brother was a Marine stationed in Viet Nam at that time. Yet, by 1968 it seemed that the world was falling apart in Viet Nam and in the United States. M.L. King, Jr.'s assassination followed by Robert Kennedy's assassination coupled with the worsening situation in Viet Nam blanketed the nation with a feeling of despair.

In the fall of that year, my high school counselor called me into his office, again. I would be a frequent visitor to his office that school year. My counselor was a very soft-spoken man who was interested in the students. He was undeniably the most patient person on earth, and perhaps one of the most creative and persistent high school counselors in the universe (you will see why I use the word "creative" in a moment). He knew I was at best a marginal student and at worse a student who didn't give a damn about school. He also knew my grades were terrible, but he always encouraged me to do better and he encouraged me to come by anytime to talk to him.

My counselor told me that if I took a real class in place of Study Hall and completed research papers for a Social Studies class, an English class, and a World History class that I had failed during my Junior year and passed all of my current classes I could graduate a year later than I should have, because I dropped out of school for a while (more on that later). I recollected that I failed more than those classes and the prospect of passing all of my current classes made his analysis dubious. But his plan was better than my plan to drop out of school, again, and join the military. After all, the Vietnam War was raging at that time so remaining in school seemed like a more prudent option.

In one of life's unexpected turns, I was moved from Study Hall to an Art class, which was the only class other than Physical Education where all students could be together regardless of their Level status. In the Art class, I met a girl, an exceptionality pretty, smart, and artistically talented eleventh-grade student. She was the type of girl who was unintentionally intimidating to guys because of her looks and brains. We became very good friends–I guess opposites do attract. She was the type of person who saw the best in people and thrived in a school setting. She was a gifted student who was challenged academically in her classes, and she loved the challenge. Her public education was topnotch. She later received two college degrees. She encouraged me and even worked on the research papers I had to do for the previously mentioned classes. Best of all for me, she became my tutor, confidant, and my best friend.

Other than my Earth Science teacher in high school, my Art teacher was one of the few high school teachers who encouraged students, made a concerted effort to motivate students, talked and listened to students and who never had any discipline problems in her classroom – the latter being notable considering the mix of students in the class. Maybe she was influenced by Carl Rogers' book *Freedom to Learn* that was published during that time. Rogers had the audacity to insist that students have feelings and those feelings can be "damaged" by teachers. He wrote,

I deeply believe that traditional teaching is an almost completely futile, wasteful, overrated function in today's changing world. It is successful mostly in giving children who can't grasp the material, a sense of failure. It also succeeds in persuading students to drop out when they realize that the material taught is almost completely irrelevant to their lives. No one should ever be trying to learn something for which one sees no relevance. No child should ever experience the sense of failure imposed by our grading system, by criticism and ridicule from teachers and others, by rejection when he or she is slow to comprehend.

The Art teacher not only showed the human and humane side of teaching and learning and the power of a positive classroom climate, much as Rogers advocated, but she also tried to make education seem relevant to our lives. She talked about the importance of art throughout history and how people respond to art. She showed us the relationship between mankind's civility and appreciation and development of the arts.

If a student had difficulty finding a medium that he or she could work within the art, she spent considerable time helping that student find something he could do, something he could create, something that was fun. She also recognized that students can learn a lot from other students. The artistically talented students were glad to help the other students learn about and try different methods and styles of artwork. The teacher explained how art can be a means to express a wide range of emotions, from anger to elation. Some kids simply had no clue or talent for art, so the teacher paired those students with other students who had talent and together they worked on team projects. It worked well for both students. The talented students were good and patient teachers, and the less talented students took pride in the final projects. The teacher took pictures of everyone's work in class. She had an entire wall covered with pictures of her student's artwork from previous classes. The classroom climate was engaging, and students felt connected.

Carl Rogers wrote:

I feel that our educational institutions are in a desperate state; and that unless our schools can become exciting, fun-filled centers of learning, they are quite possibly doomed.

The art teacher understood Carl Rogers, but she understood him at an intuitive level – it was her personality and her understanding of and concern for students that made her an effective teacher. She also understood the dynamics of a positive classroom climate.

Rogers changed many attitudes about teaching throughout his career and many of his insights continued far beyond his life, and today there is a reawakening of his concepts through the focus on a positive school climate and socio-emotional learning. However, too many of today's educators focus on "research-based" practices, as if this implies a new enlightened era. Rogers' conclusions were also based on research, a fact that few want to recognize or choose to remember. Rogers cited one study in particular to support his perspective.

In a study involving 600 teachers and 10,000 students, the students (from kindergarten to grade twelve) of teachers who were trained to offer high levels of empathy, congruence, and positive regard were compared with control students of teachers who did not offer high levels of these facilitative conditions. The students of the high facilitative teachers were found to:

1. Miss fewer days of school during the year.
2. Have increased scores on self-concept measures, indicating more positive self-regard.
3. Make greater gains on academic achievement measures, including both math and reading scores.
4. Present fewer disciplinary problems.
5. Commit fewer acts of vandalism to school property.
6. Make gains in creativity scores from September to May.
7. Are more spontaneous and use higher levels of thinking.

These seven results are what every public school should strive for and they can be translated into providing a positive learning climate in the classrooms and school-wide. They should be part of each public school's strategic plan, and the map leading them to these results derive from teachers with empathy, congruence, and a positive attitude.

The theme of quality education being tied to quality teaching recurs throughout the history of public education and applies today. One of the ironies and tragedies of public education is that the kids who benefit the most from empathy, congruence, and positive reinforcement are typically the students who seldom receive any. Rogers, I am certain, did not imply or believe that the combination of the academic and the effective was only for the best and the brightest.

The year 1969 was a momentous year, filled with very unlikely and improbable events: man landed on the moon, Sesame Street is broadcast on public television, the first automatic teller machine was installed, and I returned to and graduated from high school.

On July 20, 1969, I sat with my parents watching Walter Cronkite tell the world that a man was about to walk on the moon. A few minutes later there were grainy images on our little black and white television of Neil Armstrong stepping onto the moon's surface. It was a breathtaking moment. My father and I were talking about the event as a good sign that the nation was perhaps turning in a more positive direction.

Public education benefitted or should have from the attention on the lunar landing because science became relevant and United States education regained some respect. After all, we caught up with and even surpassed the Soviet Union – remember Sputnik a few years earlier.

Public education was impacted also that year with the United States Supreme Court case of *Tinker v. Des Moines Independent School District* when the Court ruled that students have First Amendment rights. The case centered on high school students who were wearing armbands to protest the Viet Nam war and were suspended out of school. This Court ruling had a major impact on public education, and it ushered in the era of student rights. A divided United States Supreme Court ruled on three main points that had a shocking effect on schools in that era and since:

1. *In wearing armbands, the petitioners were quiet and passive. They were not disruptive and did not impinge upon the rights of others. In these circumstances, their conduct was within the protection of the Free Speech Clause of the First Amendment and the Due Process Clause of the Fourteenth.*

2. *First Amendment rights are available to teachers and students, subject to application considering the special characteristics of the school environment.*

3. *A prohibition against expression of opinion, without any evidence that the rule is necessary to avoid substantial interference with school discipline or the rights of others, is not permissible under the First and Fourteenth Amendments.*

The United States Supreme Court decision was one of the first in a series of rulings that would forever impact public education. "Impact" does not adequately describe what these cases did to public education. Public education would be changed forever due to a series of Supreme Court rulings. It was described by some experts as the beginning of an "enlightened era" for the treatment of students in public school. That was an optimistic view that was not very grounded in the reality of the public-school world at the classroom level until many years later.

In the meantime, for example, many students were still being suspended or expelled from school without being told how long they were suspended or for what reason. Currently, most school districts are much more attuned to and protective of student rights.

PART THREE
SELF JOURNEY BACK

CHAPTER 13
DROPPING OUT TO DROP BACK IN

Experience is that marvelous thing that enables you to recognize a mistake when you make it again.

—Franklin P. Jones

In my small world there were a series of miracles and several angels. Remember what Gladwell wrote in *Outliers*, *"They just need a chance."* The smart girl led me through the research papers and my high school counselor weaved his creative magic and sure enough, I was in line to finally graduate.

My sojourn as a high school dropout lasted eight months and was filled with a litany of scrub jobs, encounters with law enforcement and a cast of characters, deceiving my mother, and pushing against life to see where and when and how often and how hard life would push back. It always pushed back very hard and very often.

During that lost period of time in my life, a juvenile judge sent me to a minimum-security work camp for several days because I violated probation and because of a smartass comment I made to the judge in court. My comment to the judge during court confirms that I wasn't the smartest kid around. The judge leaned over his bench and said, *"You're not as tough as you think you are and I'll prove it to you. I'm sending you to an adult work camp so you can see the other side of what is waiting for you if you don't shape up."*

He was right. That experience got my attention. He sent me to a low-security work camp for adults who could not afford to pay a fine or who had to serve "soft" time for misdemeanors. The men of various ages would arise from their camp-like cottages, eat an egg sandwich, climb aboard a truck and do highway cleaning work all day regardless of the weather. These were the infamous highway crews that were prevalent across the south. I did not stay at the work camp overnight because I was the only juvenile assigned to the work crew. Instead, my father had to bring me to the camp every morning in time to board the truck, and then he would pick me up at dusk. We worked from sunup to sundown on back-breaking highway cleaning jobs. We had a few water breaks during the day and soggy peanut butter sandwiches for lunch on the side of the road. This was an adult work camp, so I was separated from the adults. In fact, I had my own guard.

For those who remember the movie *Cool Hand Luke*, you can picture my guard. He wore a straw hat, dark sunglasses, and he carried a shotgun. There was no doubt that he meant business and his business was no nonsense. During that time in my life, adults found it difficult to get my attention, but this guard got my attention the first day. He said to me without any emotion, "Son, don't even think about messing with me because you see if you do f--k around with me your mama's going to have to buy two caskets 'cause I'll blow you in half with this shotgun." What a great line – "two caskets" - and it got my attention without a doubt because he meant it. In fact I think he was hoping I'd make a run for it so he could blow me in half. His finger was always on the trigger.

When my father picked me up, I collapsed in his truck. I was often too tired to even eat dinner. After two weeks in the work camp, I was sent back before the judge who gave me this option: return to school or return to the work camp. High school never sounded so good. I went back to school, which could have been an embarrassing moment for me, except for an unlikely event.

During my self-imposed exile, by chance, I met a police officer, a motorcycle cop. I had stopped by the local drug store to see if they were hiring and a police officer was on his motorcycle in front of the store. This was on a weekday around noon. When I stepped out of the drug store he asked me why I was not in school – was I skipping class? I told him I was not in school –I'd dropped out. We talked for a while. He was very nice, respectful and he gave me several reasons why I should return to school. I thanked him and we went our separate ways. This same officer happened to be in juvenile court the day I returned there to hear the judge's choices after my work camp experience. For whatever reason the officer took an interest in me and visited my high school the same week I returned to school.

My counselor got me out of class one day and there sat the officer in my counselor's office. We talked for a while and he said he would come by the school periodically to check on me. This was an unusual situation because "mentoring" was not common then. But he played a significant role in keeping me in school because I looked forward to talking to the officer. I can tell anyone the value of a mentor; I experienced it myself. The other students thought it was cool that I had a "cop" visiting me at school, so I saved face when I returned to school.

The police officer visited me every week for a year and kept up with me during my trials and tribulations entering the various types of menial jobs. He was delighted when he learned that I was in college. The police officer would distinguish himself throughout his career. He was described as a "cop's cop." He received many awards and became the police chief of the largest force in the state, a position he held for many years. In fact, the police headquarters in the county is named after him.

When I returned to school, I struggled mightily but had the good luck to have a friend who cared about me; a counselor who cared about me, and a police officer who cared about me. I know most people have heard of "social promotions" from one grade to the next even though the student does not do well academically. I received a "Social Graduation." I am still not exactly sure how I earned enough credits to graduate. I do know that my friend in the art class helped me with a lot of school work and papers.

Having performed miserably in high school and having failed a basic physical exam for the military due to arthritis (more on that later), all that was left for me to do was work, and I was not very good at that either.

I applied for several jobs, but I was intimidated by jobs that required skills, such as the use of a cash register, or selling anything. I was not suited for any of those. I was more suited being a gas station attendant – pump the gas, take the money, and wait for the next customer. I was offered a job at a retail store but when I went to training, I was totally intimidated by the cash register. The trainer, who was actually very good, kept telling us that we had to smile all the time. I was not coordinated enough to work the cash register and smile at the same time. I decided I was more suited for manual labor. I was for the first time beginning to worry about my future.

Finally, I found a job at a manufacturing plant. I had a lot of time to contemplate my future as I sat on a metal stool putting nuts and bolts together for commercial electrical fuse boxes. I had a job where I literary put nuts and bolts together as they ran past me on a narrow conveyor belt for ten hours a day. A cash register was a mystery to me, but I could put nuts and bolts together.

I was officially an "assembly line worker," according to the union boss. This was a very interesting experience that had an impact on decisions I would make about my future. The work was not back-breaking, but mind-breaking. The only break from this mind-killing task was the much sought-after trip to the vat that held the completed task, which was consummated when a line worker's large plastic bucket was filled with coupled nuts and bolts. In other words, the highlight of the day, other than the short breaks, was when we had the chance to get off of the metal stool to empty our ten-gallon plastic bucket filled with nuts and bolts into the gigantic vat at the back corner of the plant. We had to note each bucket by using the "clicker" that was attached to the vat. That way, the company knew how many buckets each employee was filling and emptying each day.

I was well into my third week working there before I even noticed fully the people who sat around me at the assembly line. There were young and old people with bland and blank expressions who seldom spoke a word or even acknowledged each other's existence. No human exchange took place even during the morning and afternoon ten-minute breaks. My morning greetings were met with complete silence, so after a week I sank into the assembly line silence, too. Lunch break, all twenty minutes of it, was spent in the prison-gray break room filled with more silence than dialogue. A small radio crackling with static tried in earnest to break the silence, to add some humanity to the scene, but it did not work very well. The only sound came from the outside where the smokers gathered. We did not have "no smoking" sections. It was simply the choice of smokers to be outside. It was a horrible workplace climate.

After a while the grayness of the break room and the bleakness of the employees made it seem like the employees in the break room were beginning to blend into the walls. Their greyish skin color I noticed one day in a frightening moment of observation was the same color as the walls. Thereafter, I spent my 20 minutes outside, regardless of the weather and despite the fact I didn't smoke. I spent a good part of my days there convincing myself that I could not have a life drifting from one menial job to another, but I could not stay there. I concluded I could not work on the assembly line much longer before I went crazy and started doing abnormal things like emptying my bucket before it was full.

No matter how miserable I was on the job, the fact remained that I needed the job. My parents were working all hours of the day and night just to make ends meet and so my observations of my work life were of little importance when survival was at stake. Some moments, however, clearly reveal a decision time.

My epiphany came one day during a mindless moment of a mindless day of a mindless week when I slinked off my stool to empty my bucket in the open-mouthed vat of nuts and bolts, only to have the old man sitting next to me say softly but firmly, "*Your bucket ain't full.*" For a moment I did not know if he was referring to my mental capacity, my prospects, my attention span, or my actual bucket. It became quickly apparent that his focus was my bucket. He didn't care anything about me; he only cared about the damn bucket. That was it; the proverbial slap in the face. The realization that in a few more months I would be just like him–trapped in a mind that was only stimulated to life by a bucket that was not full of nuts and bolts. I emptied my half-filled bucket, tossed the cursed bucket in the vat and walked out. I did not return.

I was facing a real dilemma. I could not go home and tell my parents I quit my job. That was totally and completely unacceptable. In fact, I could not go home until I had another job firmly in hand. You do not walk into a working-class house and say, "*Guess what, I quit my job because my bucket wasn't full.*" The same day I emptied my bucket for the last time I started my next promising career at a plastics factory.

Plastic. In the legendary movie *The Graduate*, the protagonist, Benjamin, was given some insider information that plastic was the best bet for future investments. Everything will be made of or sealed in plastic, his advisor said. He was right.

Until that time, I never really thought about the origin of plastic milk cartons and plastic wrappings and other plastic-related products. It did not take long for me to learn that we should be more appreciative of all of the factory workers who make and work with plastics-related products.

I just knew I had found my place in the industry. This was my future. Benjamin the Graduate and I would be in the plastics business. Even the fact that I was hired on the spot with no interview or background check did not hinder my enthusiasm. I thought this must be a job with complexity and one that called for a sharp mind and quick reflexes because the training for this new challenging job lasted ten whole minutes compared to the mere two-minute training I had with nuts and bolts and buckets.

The most memorable part of the training was the last part, which including the following fine points: *"(1) Don't let the hot plastic touch your skin; (2) If it does touch your skin, don't shake it or try to wipe it off; and (3) If hot plastic does touch your skin immediately run to the nearest cold water sink."*

As I would soon learn, there was a very good reason for all three of the finer points in my training. I quickly became the Poster Boy for all the tortuous ways hot plastic can cause pain and suffering. What the training did not clarify was part two of the final warning: *"Don't shake it or try to wipe the hot plastic off your skin."* The training did not clarify why one should not attempt to shake or wipe hot plastic off of your skin. Trying to shake off the hot plastic serves only to spread the misery to other parts of your body, namely your face and neck and arms. Wiping hot plastic off takes body hair and precious epidermis with it. It is funny what goes through one's mind when your arms are up to your shoulders in ice cold water and you are inhaling a combined smell of burned hair and skin mingled with the aroma of plastic and the pain of ice-cold water. The cold-water cools and hardens the plastic and it just falls off. That clarity would have been appreciated during the 10-minute training session. I wondered if the nuts and bolts corporation would take me back if I brought my own bucket and promised to fill it to the top for the rest of my life.

CHAPTER 14
COMMUNITY COLLEGES SOAR

Luck affects everything. Let your hook always be cast.
In the stream where you least expect it, there will be fish.

-Ovid

For some curious reason, the bright and beautiful girl who I met in the high school Art class during my senior year still wanted to be my friend even though she was attending a small community college on a scholarship while I was in the nuts and bolts and plastics industries. She received academic scholarship offers from other colleges and universities but her father was gravely ill, and she did not want to be far away from home. When he passed a couple of years later, she learned that a major university held a scholarship for her. She attended there and graduated with honors. She later received her master's degree.

After seeing what little there was left of the skin on my arms and hands and seeing my skin slowly becoming the color of a plastic milk carton, she made the audacious, ridiculous suggestion that I seriously reconsider my future. I didn't have any plans, so she laid out some options for me. The military would have been the number one option, but my medical condition prevented that. Finally, she said that the community college would accept me because of its "Open-Door Policy," and could I enroll in the community college with her. I did not know her to have a cruel streak at all, so I listened longer than was normal for me to listen to anything or anybody talking such nonsense. She explained the college's Open-Door Policy, which meant that anyone could give college a try. The college president believed that every community has many "*diamonds in the rough*," as he frequently said.

I went with my friend, at her insistence, to a lecture the president gave one afternoon. He was dynamic and convincing. He was a dead ringer for Mark Twain, and he took that to heart. He often conducted a one-man show impersonating Mark Twain, and he was fabulous. He always received rave reviews.

That afternoon he appealed to those in the audience to recognize the collective talent in the community; to inspire others to "extend beyond their current reach." The college president was almost pleading for the community to take that next step up to higher education. He seemed to be saying, "*What do you have to lose?*" My right arm was sore after the lecture because my friend kept poking me in my arm with her elbow about every two minutes to emphasize points that the president was making. God Bless people in the world like her and the president. Attend the community college after dropping out of high school and then barely graduating? Absurd. Another cast of characters that were going to influence my life. I was about to experience a part of public education that altered my future.

I announced one evening to my parents that I was going to attend college. Before you judge my parents' reaction, keep in mind that my father did not have an education, because he had to work, and my mother's education ended at the eighth grade for the same reason. After losing the small family dairy business, my father taught himself how to fix and repair virtually any type of machine, so he scratched out a living and my mother continued to work on an assembly line – steady work and steady pay. So, my parents' reaction to attending college was understandable: "*Does this mean you can get a real job soon?*" To my parents, a real job meant being a plumber, a mechanic, a carpenter, an electrician–a skilled trade or working for the local government in a labor job. College was an abstract concept compared to the solid understanding of what a mechanic or plumber does.

My mother, who was always calm, gentle, graceful, loving and direct ask me how I planned to balance hot plastic with college. She knew that working the graveyard shift (midnight to eight) and attending classes during the day would not work. Either I would have more hot plastic burns, drown in one of the cold waters sinks from lack of sleep or I would flunk out of college, or maybe all of the above.

I started looking for another job, but I knew I would have to continue to work at night if I planned to try the great and ridiculous experiment of college attendance. One of my uncles worked for the county water department driving a truck. He was viewed as a stalwart member of our family because he had a "government job." He had dependable work hours, a dependable salary, a dependable pension, and a uniform. Life was good in his household. He told me that a job was available that required nothing other than "*just loading a few water meter boxes*" onto trucks each night from four in the afternoon until midnight, five days a week. The pay was better than the plastics factory and there was no danger of hot plastic scarring. I was set. Now all I had to do was enroll in college and show up for work.

The idea of attending college was so ludicrous that I found the idea intriguing. Besides, my social life was nonexistent, and I thought at least I would have the chance to be around others my age even if I was going to be humiliated and embarrassed in front of them in college classes. My first thought was that the community college would not accept me. Being rejected I could handle, but I did not want the college counselor to laugh at me when I asked about enrolling.

Open Enrollment I found out did not literally mean one could just walk into class one day at the college. There was a concept called a "process" that one had to follow before entering the hallowed grounds of higher education. The process required me to visit my former high school and secure a grade transcript from my counselor. Then I had to take said grade transcript to the college counseling center. This process seemed easy to my friend, but her concept of processes and mine were very different. Besides, she was a good student in high school while I was a recovering dropout. Getting my grade transcript was going to be a good laugh for everyone except me, and the laughter would continue when I showed the grade transcript to the college counselors, I was certain.

There is a special place in heaven for my high school counselor. He worried about me for several years. He tried every way and means possible to motivate me, to instill some seed of self-respect and effort, but nothing worked. Imagine his reaction when he saw me at his door.

"*Garry*," he almost shouted, "*What are you doing here?*" I think it crossed his mind that I really didn't graduate, and I was back for another round. I gave him a brief recap of my year in industry and stunned him when I asked for a copy of my grade transcript so I could try to enroll in the community college. He looked at me as if I was speaking in tongues. His recovery was, however, very swift. He became a jumble of energy and encouragement and joy. He kept saying, *"This is wonderful; this is just wonderful; I knew it; I just knew it."* I felt like a complete fool. Here before me was a man who for several long years tried to help me and I not only shunned his help, I even ridiculed him at times. Here was a man who looked past my immaturity, my pettiness, my sarcasm and saw in me untapped potential. Here was a counselor more excited than I was about my feeble and desperate effort to attend college. He flittered around his office like his hair was on fire. He told me to sit and wait for him while he made of copies of my grade transcript. He also told the other counselors who quickly gathered at his office door like they were expecting me to say something or do something. They were all excited. Who were these people? They were acting like the president had pardoned me and canceled the execution.

Like magic, my counselor had before him my sorry academic record. I had never seen such a mess. To receive bad grades one quarter at a time does not portray the full picture of one's ineptitude. There were no A's, only a couple of B's, some C's, and many D's and F's. Again, that feeling of foolishness rose in my throat. I was not even sure how all of that added up to a high school diploma and yet here I was kidding myself about college.

I have thought of that moment many times since then - about how my counselor was so reassuring and encouraging and proud that I was at least going to give life a try. I have also reflected on my own reaction at the time I saw my "permanent record." I was embarrassed. I was ashamed. It occurred to me that one's efforts and attitude do matter. It was painfully obvious that education and everything related to one's education matters.

With my counselor's encouragement still ringing in my ears and my face still flushed from embarrassment, I walked into the community college counseling center later that afternoon. It is a very sobering recollection now how close I came to missing the appointment, which would have altered my life. As I waited for a counselor, I looked at my grade transcript, again. I convinced myself then and there that the college counselor might laugh at me when she looked over my grade transcript. Her laughing at me was a very real possibility. I did not think I could handle that. The counseling waiting area seemed to shrink. The office noises seemed to grow dull and distant. My breathing became heavy and labored. This whole idea of college was absurd and based on my physical and psychological reaction it was probably dangerous, too. I stood up to leave. I actually stood up to leave. I just could not enroll in college. The idea of going to college was ludicrous. I made it to the door with heavy feet and laid my hand on the door to leave when I heard my name being called as if from a cliff on the other side of a valley. Slowly, I turned. The counselor said, "*You are Garry McGiboney, right?*" "*Well, young man where are you going?*" "*You're not trying to skip out on me, are you?*" I could not speak, so I just shook my head. Think about, which I have done many times, another five seconds or less and I would have been out the door and on my way to a life of menial jobs. God, that was close. Five seconds from nowhere. Five seconds from an uncertain life. Five seconds from obscurity. Five seconds from wondering what could have been. It is a scary thought to think across the United States at any given moment of any given day a young person is five seconds away from a decision that will alter his or her life.

The college counselor said, "*Well, good, come on in here and let's see what we can do.*" Let the laughter begin.

In her office I handed over my grade transcript much like one would offer his arm for an amputation. Bracing for the laughter, I got instead a thoughtful "*We have some work to do*" and a smile – a genuine smile. She said, "*It appears that you were not in school for a year.*" "*What happened?*" I told her I'd dropped out for a while. I didn't offer any more details. She said, "*You know, that's okay. Like I say all the time, it's the standing after a fall that matters. We can make this work if you're willing to work hard and follow the path we set for you.*" "*Are you willing to do that, Garry?*"

That "work to do" was remedial classes in Math and English - a lot of remedial classes. Essentially, I had to cover Math and English material that I did not master in high school, which meant I had to take three remedial Math classes and three remedial English classes before I qualified to take any college classes for credit. That was a full year of remedial classes. I was not sure about that. The counselor saw my reaction and immediately explained that the classes would have other people in them much like me who needed to build a stronger foundation before taking college credit classes. She made me promise that I would try. She was an angel.

I didn't know what to expect from the instructors, but the remedial Math and English instructors were great to work with. The classes were small and the interaction between the instructors and students was positive and informative. The instructors engaged with the students and learned our moods and style of learning. The instructors were sensitive to students who struggled and offered them extra time and extra assistance.

I made C's in my first remedial Math and English classes and that was with a great deal of effort. I worked hard and I studied long and hard. I was discouraged to the point of wanting to quit several times, but the instructors were instrumental in my staying with classes. They basically told me I could not quit; they wouldn't let me. The classroom's climate centered on engagement, motivation, support, encouragement, humor, and celebrations of small successes. Otherwise, I wouldn't have made it past the first month.

I had to learn the subject matter, but I also had to learn how to study, how to identify my learning style, how to take tests, to learn how to learn. It was a whole new world, a foreign world to me. I almost felt guilty because of the amount of time the instructors had to spend with me. To me, it was the equivalent of going from elementary school straight to college.

I did much better with my second tier of remedial classes, and I begin to feel like I might be able to learn some of the college stuff. With considerable and on-going help from the instructors, including after-class tutoring, I passed all of the remedial classes, even though it took a year. At the end of the year, the instructors had a class party for those who finished the course work. We were not too old to enjoy a class party because for most of us we were experiencing success for the first time, and our instructors were truly proud of us. I could never thank them enough.

After a year of remedial classes, I was finally eligible to take "real" college classes – classes for credit, which was exciting and very scary.

During my remedial year at college, I took on the job that my uncle helped me acquire. However, those "water meter boxes" my uncle talked about turned out to be cast iron commercial water meter boxes that weighed 100 pounds each. My job was to load five of these huge cast iron meter boxes into flatbed trucks, so the next morning the installation crews could take off to the job sites to install them. I had twenty trucks to load each night from 4:00 p.m. to midnight, or later if I wasn't finished. Typically, my job ended at 1:00 in the morning. If the weather was bad, it might be even later. Cold nights and 100-pound cast iron meter boxes was a tough combination.

My training was on-the-job training. I arrived early on my first day in the new job with some fear. I was taking on too much at the same time—a new job and college. A tall, thin man met me at the door and turned to walk toward the loading dock area without saying a word. I assumed that he expected me to follow him. I had nothing else to do, so I followed him. He said, "*Put five of these meter boxes in each truck over yonder.*" Then he walked to the row of trucks that had backhoes (ditch diggers) on long trailers attached to the back of the trucks. He said, "*You fill these trucks up and then you fill the backhoes up.*" I assumed he meant I should fill them up with gasoline, but I did not want to interrupt the flow of information. He walked back toward the small office area and naturally I followed him. He suddenly stopped and said, "*What are you doing?*" I just shrugged. He said, "*You'd better get to work - it'll take you all night.*"

When I reached down for the first time to lift a cast iron meter box, I was stunned by the weight. Lifting the meter boxes into each truck took a mighty effort and pumping gas into all the trucks and into the backhoes took a lot of time. My hands took a beating from the rough corners and edges of the cast iron meter boxes, even when wearing heavy insulated gloves. With the weight of the meter boxes, I mostly dragged them to the edge of the dock and tried to lower them gently into the truck bed. Cast iron is tough but on cold nights they can break. One broken meter box would be the equivalent of two days of my salary.

Trying to drive the trucks close enough to the gas pump for the hose to reach the gas tanks without getting too close and turning the entire area into a tragic fire scene was no easy task. Then I had to maneuver the truck so the gas hose could reach the backhoe gas tanks. All of this was easy compared to the most difficult task of all – backing up a five-ton truck with a backhoe trailer attached to it into a small area with just enough space between each truck for the doors to open.

There is an art to backing up a truck and trailer, and I did not have Kurt Anderson's book "*How to Back Up a Trailer*" and no one was available to show me how. How was I to know, as Anderson notes in his book, that the world is backward in the backing-up-trailer universe? If you want the trailer to go left, you turn right; if you want the trailer to go right you turn left. If you make normal turns the trailer will act like it's tired of you and try to run off into the woods. The art of backing up a trailer is to use a thousand small, incremental turns. That way if you really screw up at least the truck and trailer can be salvaged. If you turn the steering wheel in a normal fashion, the truck and trailer tend to tip over in awkward, unnatural angles, causing damage to the truck, trailer, backhoe, and meter boxes.

All this maneuvering takes place while you're looking at the side view mirrors, which puts everything in reverse order. It's a parallel but opposite universe. Another rookie mistake and false-illusion is this: if one can get the truck and trailer in a perfectly straight line by pulling forward, the driver can then back them in a straight line right into the desired parking spot. No such luck. Einstein was famous for his Theory of Relativity, but his second most famous theory was his You-Cannot-Back-up-a-Truck-and-Trailer-in-a-Straight-Line Theory because it goes against all elements of the natural world. Backing up a truck and trailer in a straight line goes against all laws of physics. No one has accomplished that feat. It can be humorous watching people trying to learn how to do it. That is exactly where my boss found his humor each afternoon and evening. I could see him standing in the doorway of this office laughing heartily at my misadventures backing trucks and trailers into the designated spots.

One night I was thoroughly perplexed, both at how I managed to do such a thing and next by how I was going to correct it before the sun rose the next morning. Somehow, I managed to jackknife a truck and trailer while backing it between two other trucks and trailers. How in the world does one pull off a jackknife between two other trucks? The truck was turned at an odd angle and the trailer was almost perpendicular to the trucks and trailers on either side. I had no idea how I managed to do that. When I went to the manager's office for some help he was already gone for the night – laughing all the way home, I'm sure. The only way out was to move the other trucks and trailers so I could attempt to straighten out the wayward truck and trailer and start over. I left work at about 3:00 a.m. that morning. On the way home, I wanted to drop by the plastics factory and stick my head into one of those vats of cold water.

My day at college started at 8:00 a.m. and ended at 2:00 p.m. five days a week. The instructors were kind enough to work with me after classes and then I studied until it was time to battle the trucks and trailers at 4:00 p.m. each afternoon. When I got home each night, I took a shower and then studied until about 4:00 a.m. Then up at 7:00 a.m. for classes.

It was a brutal schedule, both physically and mentally. The job wore me down physically and college worked me over emotionally and cognitively.

Even though the remedial classes were taught by caring and supportive instructors, I didn't expect the same devotion to students in the college classes. I was not prepared for the type of learning experience and school climate I encountered. Every professor and instructor at the community college showed interest in their students, encouraged dialogue and debate, did not treat student questions like an affront, and helped at every turn. I was amazed.

A funny thing happened on my path through the community college experience. I found that I enjoyed learning. I rediscovered reading. I discovered that I could learn some difficult material. I discovered that I need not be embarrassed if I had difficulty with the subject matter. I discovered that I wanted to live up to the professors' and instructors' expectations. It was a whole new world for me. It was a world of discovery and hope and positive and expectations and classroom climates.

Carl Rogers in his book *Freedom to Learn* described the ideal classroom conditions for learning.

In the classrooms of teachers who were more empathic, more congruent, and more respectful of their students, there was:

1. *More student talk*
2. *More student problem solving*
3. *More verbal initiation*
4. *More verbal response to a teacher*
5. *More asking of questions*
6. *More involvement in learning*
7. *More eye contact with the teacher*
8. *More physical movement*
9. *Higher levels of cognition*
10. *Greater creativity*

In addition, these benefits were cumulative; the more years in succession that students had a high functioning teacher, the greater the gains when compared with students of low functioning teachers.

These ten outcomes were obvious across the campus at the community college due to the compassion, enthusiasm, positive classroom and college climate, support, and motivation of the college's professors. It was interesting that the high school I attended lacked what was at the community college–teachers with skills and the ability to engage students, a positive learning climate, high expectations, and care and concern at multiple levels.

CHAPTER 15
PRIDE AGAINST PREJUDICE

Who in the world am I? Ah, that's the great puzzle.

—Lewis Carroll

Ivan Illich published *De-schooling Society* in the 1970s era and wrote,

> *Many students, especially those who are poor, intuitively know what the schools do for them. They school them to confuse process and substance. Once these become blurred, a new logic is assumed: the more treatment there is, the better are the results; or, escalation leads to success. The pupil is thereby "schooled" to confuse teaching with learning, grade advancement with education, a diploma with competence, and fluency with the ability to say something new.*

The assault on public education continued from many different perspectives. Rist echoed many of the concerns of the era when he wrote,

> *Within the framework of labeling theory...a major emphasis has been placed upon the role of [academic] institutions in sorting, labeling, tracking, and channeling persons along various routes depending upon the assessment the institution has made of the individual.*

Public education was under a microscope and under fire at the same time and from several different sources in the 1970s. While some in public education were quick to try any and all new fads, many other educators circled the wagons of defense and defiance. The difference between the two responses was probably couched in the expectations of public education at the local level. There was a strong sentiment that public education provided stability in an otherwise unpredictable world. Still, others looked deep into public education and found it lacking. This polarization of public education mutated into a political tool. Public education in the 1970s and since has become the experimental laboratory for social and political ideology, a cottage industry for educational fads and materials, and a money-maker for consultants with the latest and greatest "approach" to education.

While issues in K-12 public education were debated, life in community colleges was beginning to flourish as people from all backgrounds found an education home. The purpose of community colleges, a uniquely American concept, was based on the needs of students and, consequently, was shaped by those needs.

As I mentioned, by community college professors were good, caring individuals. They were tough and fair, and they kept up a relentless pace. They were very demanding but very specific in how to meet the demands. This was not one of those experiences you find in a public four-year college where 200 students in a class find a clear image of a fuzzy concept on a daily basis with a tenured professor who may or may not show up for the majority of the classes. Community colleges are different and are more successful at turning students around. Here is an example.

One day after a befuddling English class, at least befuddling to me, the English professor stopped me as I was leaving her class. This was my first class for college credit after a year of remedial classes. I was intimidated as soon as I walked into the classroom. The professor had a very professional, no-nonsense appearance and demeanor, not in a cold or aloof manner, just very professional and she was beautifully articulate. She had an expansive vocabulary that would impress anybody and everybody. Even though she was not an intimidating person intentionally, she was an imposing and impressive person. She had taught for several years at a major research university as a full professor and retired from that position and moved to Atlanta to be close to her grandchildren. She took a part-time position at the community college.

Before I got to the classroom door, she asked me if I was struggling. I guess the look on my face gave me away. I paused and simply nodded my head. I thought she would probably say something like *"College is not for everyone,"* but she did not. Instead, she said I could come by her office after class to see if she could assist me or if she could find another student to work with me. I quickly accepted her offer. I guess she was probably surprised that I became such a frequent visitor to her office. In fact, I went by her office almost every day after class. I even sought her assistance with other classes. When I told her I needed a little extra help with math, she arranged for another student to help me. She even participated in discussions with me about economics and philosophy that helped me understand concepts.

She quietly helped many students like me. She was officially a part-time professor, but in reality, she was a full-time teacher, mentor, advocate, and tutor. If I was not successful in college because I could not do the work, she could only go so far with that, and we both knew that without it ever being discussed but she wanted to make sure that I at least had the chance. I admired her good heart, her encouragement, and her intelligence so much that soon I was very motivated to do the best I could. I did not want to disappoint her. I wish I had expressed more fully to her how much of a difference she made in my life and how she restored my confidence.

I had several other excellent professors at the community college. Many people minimize or marginalize or even ridicule community colleges, but if they do, they do not know the facts. In many places on many community college campuses and in the heart of many college graduates, it is evident that community colleges provide a quality public education. When compared to students who enter four-year colleges as a freshman, a freshman who completes a community college curriculum and then transfer to a four-year college is more likely to earn an undergraduate degree. Community colleges are student-centered; that's why they are successful.

Here is an example of student-centered. I was eating a quick snack between classes one day when I thought I heard soft crying nearby. I stopped to listen, and it seemed like the sound was coming from a small stand of trees surrounded by scrubs. I walked over slowly and saw a young girl crying. I deliberately and softly cleared my throat and said, *"Oh, excuse me. I didn't mean to disturb you. I was just looking for a place to sit."* She looked up through pale green eyes. With tears streaming down her face I noticed that she did not look at me; she looked at my food.

I asked if she was ok. She just nodded. I said, *"Do you want to share this sandwich with me? It's from the snack bar and I haven't opened it."* She nodded her head, again. I gave her my sandwich. She looked at me and said, *"Are you sure it's okay?"* She was starving. As we talked, I learned that she had to hitch rides to classes, and it took all of her minimum wage salary at a nearby retail store to pay for her apartment rent, books, and tuition. She lived on her own since her parents died three years previously while on a mission trip to Guatemala. She had no siblings, no uncles, and her only aunt lived in another state. She didn't say it, but she was crying because she was hungry. And I thought I had it rough.

After she ate and cleaned her face, I asked her to go with me to the counseling center. She was reluctant; she protested that she didn't need counseling. I finally convinced her that they may have some resources for her. When we arrived, I asked to speak to the counselor who saved me. I gave her some background on the young woman, and she said, *"Oh, my goodness, we have a lot of things we can do to help her; bring her in."* I didn't stay so I don't know exactly what was done, but I couple of weeks later I heard someone yelling behind me, *"Hey, wait; I need to talk to you."* It was the same young woman. She ran up to me and gave me a mighty hug. She said, *"Thank you so much. The counselor gave me a food voucher – free food – that she will renew each semester. Her daughter is my size so she brought me some of the nicest clothes I've ever seen. And I now attend her church where everyone is offering to help me. I had no idea people could be so understanding and helpful."* It's called a community college because it is a community of caring people.

Do you believe in miracles or the power of hope? Do you believe in helping others? Only a few years after a public-school K-12 experience that almost produced another dropout, I graduated from the community college. As I said earlier, I spent my first year taking remedial courses, but I made the Dean's List each of my last two years at the community college. I was the first college graduate in my family. My parents were working and could not attend the graduation, but my high school counselor, several friends, my college counselor, and my math tutor attended. The college professor who worked tirelessly with me after class also attended. I was very proud of myself, but I was equally touched knowing what it felt like to live up to the expectations of people I admired and who had given me so much of their time.

Something more must be said about the uniquely American concept of public community colleges and how they have changed and continue to change many lives. The history of community colleges, which is a uniquely American concept, dates to the Truman Commission report in 1947. The Commission report recommended a network of community colleges throughout the United States where students could attend colleges that are affordable and that are in the local communities. The GI bill offered college tuition for soldiers but many of them could not find a college nearby.

The Commission recognized the value of making college more accessible to more citizens and soldiers. To this day most people do not grasp the importance of community colleges. Some four-year higher education supporters look down their collective noses at community colleges, possibly because community college growth is outpacing four-year college growth, but that opinion may be changing.

In his book *Big Man on Campus*, the long-time and legendary president of George Washington University, Stephen Tractenberg, wrote the following:

> *There are people who go to community colleges for two years and then transfer to four-year institutions and do as well as or better than others who did their freshman and sophomore years on four-year campuses. This might indicate that the experience they had in the two-year colleges prepared them as well as or even better than those who went to the four-year undergraduate institution from the onset.*

Also, four-year colleges often give priority to students transferring from community colleges, citing their demonstrated preparedness for junior and senior college-level work. The community college I attended, for example, had "Transfer Admission Guarantees" (TAG) agreements with 30 four-year colleges in the state and in other states, because the four-year colleges found that the community college students do well in their colleges after receiving an Associate degree at a community college.

If America wants to promote higher education and if parents want their children to attend college, the "diamond in the rough" is America's public community colleges. If public schools want to see effective teaching and student success, they need not look any further than the closest public community college. If the leaders of public education want to measure the pulse of education in public high schools, turn to the instructors, professors, and counselors in community colleges. Collectively, they can tell where the strengths, weaknesses, and gaps are in public high school education, more so than their four-year college counterparts. The community college staff members see the faces of each student and to them, each student matters.

Too often local school districts and state education agencies tend to focus more if not exclusively on collaboration with four-year colleges. As an example, the community college I attended with three campuses did not receive the attention or effort at collaboration from the local public school district, even though that school district struggled for years with poor student academic performance. Instead, the local school district tried to court four-year colleges and universities. Over the years, various local superintendents held breakfast meetings, retreats and private meetings with the major universities while overlooking the local public community college. Other than an occasional project or program, the collaboration with major universities was always disappointing. Yet, just around the corner, a community college waited with open arms and a very successful record with students from all walks of life.

Some school districts have developed a seamless relationship with community colleges, even to the point of sharing teachers and resources, but there is rich potential for more partnerships of this type that would greatly enhance public education.

After my community college experience, I took my new-found confidence and my cast iron water meter box body to a four-year university, a major urban research university. The university began as an "evening college" for those who had to work while attending college. One of the classroom buildings is a former parking deck that was filled in and remodeled as a building. Class registration at one time was held at the local municipal auditorium. The university grew very rapidly and has now become a major urban research institution with an enrollment of over 50,000 students, which makes it one of the largest in the nation.

My acceptance into the university was due to my success at the community college. Nevertheless, the thought of attending the university was very intimidating. Just getting to classes would be a challenge – navigating through downtown traffic for morning classes. I could not afford a dorm. I was living in an "efficiency basement apartment." An "efficiency basement apartment" means a very inexpensive subterranean dwelling with a musty smell, no windows, unreliable indoor plumbing, and only two central heating and air conditioning thermostat settings – hot and cold.

I knew that the classes at the university would have double or triple the number of students than in my community college classes. Also, I knew it would be very unlikely that any professor at a four-year college would have any interest in my success or struggles compared to the community college setting.

When Rosenthal and Jacobson wrote *Pygmalion in the Classroom* the focus was on the role of expectations in public education at the elementary and secondary level. Interestingly, many college professors and administrators apparently did not think this concept of expectations applied to the college level or to the business world, but Dov

Eden's *Pygmalion in Management* changed that perception to a certain extent. Apparently, the self-fulfilling prophecy based on expectations applies to many settings, including college, particularly public colleges and universities.

When I started taking classes at the university, I expected to be successful and it was the primary job of the professors, in my naïve opinion, to prevent that opinion from changing. The expectation of success through effort was apparently instilled in me while I attended the community college. My point here is that the power of expectations applies to many settings and situations.

A well-documented study from 1900 tells the story of the Hollerith tabulating machine newly installed at the United States Census Bureau in 1890. The machine worked something like the typewriter with punch cards and required workers to learn a new skill the inventor regarded as complex. The punch cards were fed into cash registers and other calculation devices to speed the work. The inventor Herman Hollerith told a group of workers that the machine was very complicated and difficult to operate; consequently, he estimated that trained workers would be able to process only 550 punch cards per day if they could handle the stress of a complicated task and production requirements.

After initial training and two weeks of experience the workers were producing 550 punch cards per day, and after a period of time they produced a few more, but only at great emotional cost and extra time at work. Soon thereafter, 200 new workers were added. They went through the same standardized training on the machine, but they were NOT told that the machine was complicated and difficult to operate, and they were not given a quota for production. The new workers knew nothing of the stress and strain experienced and expressed by the other group and heard nothing about the number of punch cards expected to be produced per day. In other words, there was no set of limitations or restrictive expectations. While the original group of workers was wringing themselves out to produce 600 punch cards per day, the new group soon began tabulating 2,100 per day with no ill effects. Expectations work both ways.

I guess, by analogy, I fell into the second group in the Hollerith Study because I did not know that four-year college experience was supposed to be painful and stressful. Also, entering as a junior helped me avoid the classes with 300 or more students that typically await freshmen and sophomores. I don't know if I could have managed that.

While the professors were interesting and focused on the course material, they were not as student-centered as I was used to at the community college. Still, the professors found time to meet with students if so requested. I met a few times with professors with follow-up questions about assignments or papers. Each professor was generous with their time and very helpful. Their personalities and offices were each uniquely different. Some were almost shy and had few personal items in their office and some were gregarious and the office looked like home.

As I waited to see a professor one afternoon, I became concerned about meeting with him and getting to work on time. As the minutes ticked away, suddenly I heard a scream from the professor's office. I stood up and looked around to see if anyone else heard it, but no one was nearby. I wasn't sure what to do. Just as I turned to look for a security officer the professor's door burst open. The professor and a student were laughing out loud. After the other student left, I was invited into his office. He said, "*I guess you're wondering what the noise was all about. That student came to me to drop out of my class because he had the pressures of work, a disability, financial issues, and a full course load.*" The professor invited me to sit down. "*But we talked a long time and I told him some stories about my whacky family and how many things I had to overcome to reach my goals. When I told him I had to dress up like a woman in a play that paid me $10 per night, he erupted in laughter, because as you see I'm 6-6" and 275 pounds.*" We both laughed. What's important to me was the fact the professor spent a great deal of his time to convince a student to remain in his class, to fight through adversity, and find humor to keep the dark moments at bay. The professor did not have to devote that time to the student. But he did because he cared, and that student passed the course.

I had my share of stressful moments, like being late to classes because of various calamities and setbacks with work, cars, and bills, but the entire experience was rewarding and successful even though it was very difficult to attend school as a full-time student while working at a full-time job, but many people manage it.

My undergraduate interest was in psychology, but I soon realized that the job market for freshly minted undergraduates with a psychology degree was dry; therefore, under the advice of a college career counselor, I took enough education classes to become certified to teach. That was Plan B. I never wanted to be or intended to be a teacher. After all, why should I consider working in a public school? My personal experiences in the public K-12 world were not very pleasant and I did not want to have anything to do with that atmosphere, but the lure of a possible job trumped my foreboding about working in public education.

My college psychology classes were very difficult and deliciously challenging. We learned about the traditional theories of everyone from William James, the father of psychology, to Sigmund Freud and his obsession with sexual ideation, but we also studied the more non-traditional psychological theories and we were encouraged to avoid dogma and instead to think creatively when studying or working with people and their problems or challenges. Probably the most important "skill" was learning how to listen to others. It was an important lesson to learn. When we were videotaped interviewing various people, the video showed every student in the classes talked more than the "client" by two-thirds, but when asked afterward each student predicted that the exchange was 75% client talking. We were all surprised when we viewed our video interviews.

In the College of Education, I had a strange selection of classes on curriculum, classroom design, a class on how children learn to read, a class entitled Educational Foundation, which was a history of public education, and a few other classes that were noteworthy more for what they did not cover than what they did cover.

The study of curriculum was very big at the university, but the more obvious teacher survival skills such as classroom management, school climate development, problem-solving, how to conduct a parent conference, how to read and understand standardized assessments, and the psychological and physiological development of children were absent from the course selection. As I would experience, these were available to graduate students, but not undergraduate students majoring in education and planning to teach in public schools. and even in graduate school, these topics were more often available in graduate psychology classes than in education graduate classes.

There was a discernable difference of opinion between the education professors and the psychology professors regarding public education and the human factor. The psychology professors discussed the practical application of research on behavior, such as motivation, while the educator professors showed little interest or dismissed the relationship between motivation/ expectations and student performance. To the education professors, it was all about teaching with no discussion about the condition of students – poverty, physical and psychological conditions or the climate of schools. To the education professors, it was *"Johnny can't read because the curriculum is weak, the teacher's skills are weak, or the student has a learning disability."* To the psychology professors, it was *"Johnny can't read because he's not motivated, his home is not conducive to learning, he's hungry, he's angry, he's depressed, he's lonely, he's going through stages of psychological changes, and the school climate is negative."*

Education professors had an opinion about how public education should operate and the psychology professors had a different opinion about how public education should operate when the truth of it all is that few if any of the professors had ever worked in a public school or conducted research in a public school and if they had worked in a public school it was back at the turn of the previous century.

There was very little preparation of teachers in college for the real world of public education. Prospective teachers needed to understand how schools operate, how children grow physically and psychologically, how children learn, how children react to various situations, how teaching is multi-faceted and complex, the importance of school and classroom climate, plus many more areas of child development.

While I was navigating the differences of opinion between psychology professors and education professors regarding human behavior and motivation in my own little world and mind, a book was published that clearly showed the difference between the world view of education professors and psychology professors.

Harvard Professor Christopher Jencks confirmed that public education classrooms are the laboratory for social and political discussion. A social, educational and political firestorm broke over his very controversial book *Inequality: A Reassessment of the Effect of Family and Schooling in America*.

Jencks opined that it is probably wiser to define a "good" school in terms of student body characteristics than in terms of the budget or school resources or quality of instruction. According to Jencks, who supported in part the *Coleman Report* (the study that argued school funding has little effect on student achievement and that student background and socioeconomic status are much more important in determining educational outcomes than are measured differences in school resources), once a good school starts taking in "undesirable" students (the definition of desirable sometimes pertains to academic, social, or economic attributes), its academic standing automatically declines. He concluded that while an elementary school's social composition had only a moderate effect on student cognitive achievement, secondary or high school social composition had a significant effect on achievement. Jencks also concluded that school racial composition had only a small effect on black students' later occupational status. Therefore, his findings were interpreted to mean that the integration of schools would not benefit all students.

My psychology professors expressed outrageous indignation toward Jencks and his conclusions. The book was required reading and the professors encouraged debate and discussion about his book. What was the view and opinion of the professors in the education classes? Not a word, not a note of recognition that any of them ever read the book or even knew of the book. It was clear that teacher training was *Semper eadem*-always the same.

CHAPTER 16
PRIMUM NON NOCERE

You know there is a problem with the education system when you realize that out of the 3 R's only one begins with an R."

-Dennis Miller

The *semper eadem* approach to teaching was seriously challenged by a new and interesting philosophy about teaching expounded by the legendary Maxine Green in her book *Teacher as Stranger*, a landmark work which promoted the idea of the reflective practitioner before it became fashionable:

If the teacher agrees to submerge himself into the system, if he consents to be defined by others' views of what he is supposed to be then he gives up his freedom to see, to understand and to signify for himself.

Greene advocated the idea that teachers need a fresh view of their role as if viewing it from the perspective of a stranger, in order to be a better teacher and a more enlightening and complete person. Her "stranger" view encourages teachers to explore the idea of being more thoughtful about teaching, to consider habits, routines, practices as a stranger-as-observer would.

To take a stranger's point of view on everyday reality is to look inquiringly and wonderingly on the world in which one lives. It is like returning home from a long stay in some other place. The homecomer notices details and patterns in his environment he never saw before.

Green advocated a break from the status quo, encouraging teachers to step back and ask, "*What am I doing; why am I doing this; and is there a better way?* Greene's concepts were embraced by psychologists around the country, because the concepts were supportive of reflective interaction with others and consistent with a focus on the needs of others with the recognition that socio-emotional engagement is critical to teaching and learning. Not to the point that everyone is an equally capable or engaging, but only to the point where the idea of viewing one's behavior and the interaction with other people as one and the same, as a dynamic interaction that can either aid or hinder communications and therefore impact the effectiveness of a teacher. Teachers cannot be effective and cannot emotionally survive the rigors of teaching without "refreshing through reflection." That is how we learn to learn; that is how we broaden our view of self and others. That is how teachers can be more effective.

If he is willing to take the view of the home-comer and create a new perspective on what he has habitually considered real his teaching may become the project of a person vitally open to his students and the world...he will feel more alive than he ever has before ...there are countless lives to be changed, worlds to be remade.

This theme is one developed in three of her other texts: *Landscapes of Learning, The Dialectic of Freedom,* and

Releasing the Imagination, which is an exceptional message to teachers to use creativity and imagination in lesson planning and lesson implementation.

Greene's wonderful ideas and optimism about self-determination, self-growth, and the resulting positive influence on others could enliven the careers of many teachers and instill a powerful philosophical approach to teaching, which would benefit all students. Instead, many teachers in public education were not only unfamiliar with Greene's powerful books, they never heard of her.

The favorite description Greene uses to describe the role and perception of too many teachers is from the Greek Mythology story of Sisyphus–struggling eternally to roll the stone to the top of the hill only to have it roll back down. The struggle either incapacitates the person or the struggle becomes the purpose.

Green was the impetus for social-emotional learning and engagement movement in many schools today.

What I learned in college that shaped how I would later work with students was derived more from the psychology professors than from the education professors. That would be okay if most teachers had the psychology classes, too, but they do not. As I would witness later in my professional life, too many colleges and universities do not train teachers to be inquisitive, nurturing, enthusiastic, creative, and positive people while they are learning the principles of teaching, learning, and student performance standards, classroom climate, and assessment.

Greene has always seen the learning power of motivation, but teachers are seldom versed in human motivation other than perhaps operant conditioning (increase the likelihood of specific behavior by deliberate control of positive or negative reinforcement – see the works of B.F. Skinner).

Sometimes the theories of self-concept are shared with prospective teachers, but too often out of context. Self-concept is introduced to teachers as a preexisting condition of children instead of a cause and effect dynamic where teachers play a central role. Teachers are taught that self-concept is something teachers and students have to overcome instead of recognizing that self-concept is an outcome, not an input.

The key to learning for most students is the relationship with the teacher. If students do not think the teacher cares, or has the motivation to prepare for classes, or lacks the ability or willingness to "connect" with students, the potential for learning is lost because the conditions for learning are negative at worse and neutral at best. That is why school climate and classroom climate are so important. They address the conditions for learning, but there is more. Once the conditions for learning are improved, it's the natural progression to focus on a social-emotional engagement where the connectedness and engagement between the teacher and the student are natural and nurtured.

According to the Collaborative for Academic, Social, and Emotional Learning (CASEL),

Social and emotional learning (SEL) is the process through which children and adults acquire and

effectively apply the knowledge, attitudes, and skills necessary to understand and manage emotions, set and achieve positive goals, feel and show empathy for others, establish and maintain positive relationships, learn to effectively communicate with each other, and make responsible decisions.

SEL can be seamlessly integrated into a school's climate, culture, and norms or explicitly taught outside of academic learning time. The engagement helps students feel like they are part of the classroom, school, and social network at school because they interact with other students and teachers at a level that encourages more exchanges and connections. SEL includes self-awareness, self-management, social awareness, relationship skills, and responsible decision-making.

According to The Pennsylvania State University and Robert Wood Johnson Foundation research brief "Social Emotional Learning in Elementary School,"

Extensive research shows that SEL programs can promote academic achievement and positive social behavior, and reduce conduct problems, substance abuse, and emotional distress. Benefits of SEL in the elementary years have been documented in reviews by independent research teams and through meta-analyses which demonstrate the immediate and long-term positive outcomes of well-designed, well-implemented SEL programming.

Long-term, SEL improves students' attitudes toward learning, improves attitudes toward other students and teachers, and their self-efficacy. Recent and current research points to social-emotional learning as a key to reducing conflicts in school, increasing concentration on academic tasks, improving executive functioning such as better management of time, fewer overt overreactions, and more mature problem solving, which research shows improves graduation rates, increases enrollment in institutions of higher learning, provides greater capacity for workplace success, improves mental health, reduces crime, and improves the prevalence of overall healthier relationships and self-efficacy.

In a 2017 follow-up study to a 2011 SEL study, it was found that the effects of SEL continue to benefit students even years after being influenced by SEL components. According to CASEL,

In follow-up assessments, an average of 3.5 years after the last intervention, the academic performance of students exposed to SEL programs was an average 13 percentile points higher than their non-SEL peers, based on the eight studies that measured academics. SEL continued to boost student well-being in the form of greater social and emotional competencies, prosocial behavior, and prosocial attitudes. Furthermore, SEL students showed lasting decreases in negative outcomes such as conduct problems, emotional distress, and drug use, compared to control groups.

The combination of a positive school climate and SEL is a powerful impact on the lives of students and the careers of teachers.

In the same year, Steve Jobs, co-creator of Apple, Inc., drops out of Reed College in Portland, Oregon; Watergate grows into an American albatross; Bobby Fischer beats Boris Spassky; man lands on the moon for the last time; Congress passes the *Juvenile Justice and Delinquency Prevention Act* and *Public Law 94-142*, which ensures that all "handicapped" children would receive a free and public education, and I learned that I had to be a "student teacher" as part of my undergraduate degree requirements.

At the time, teacher certification candidates had to be a "student teacher" for at least one semester. When I first heard about this requirement from the career counselor, I had a flashback to that strange person setting in my high school classes.

I thought student teaching should be fairly easy since the student teacher in my high school never said a word and never did anything obvious except stare into space and occasionally write something in his ever-present notebook. However unprepared I was to actually teach, I felt prepared to interact with other people, even kids, because of the focus and the role-playing that was part of the dynamic education in the psychology department at the university.

I was about to experience public education from the deliverable instead of the receivable point of view for the first time. I had mixed emotions about the upcoming student teaching experience. Was I prepared? Would I mutate into a combination of the worst teachers I had in public school? Did I have the right frame of mind?

I was assigned to one of the finest high schools in the area. The school was well known in those days for its pool of very talented students, both academically and artistically. It was a "magnet" school, which meant students from different communities could apply to attend the school. This encouraged integration and a collection of very smart and talented students from all walks of life.

The school was a high achieving academic powerhouse, but it was also an incubator and cradle for artistic and performance talent. The productions arranged and performed by the students and staff were nothing short of professional. The director of the performing arts program was legendary and nationally known. The instructional program for the performing arts students was intensive and provided comprehensive pre-professional training while demanding the same academic standards required of non-performance students. The curriculum included music, theater, instrumental, choral, drama, dance, technical theater, and the renowned "Show Biz Kids," plus Advanced Placement academic classes.

Many graduates of the school established successful careers performing on Broadway and in movies and television. Others performed with opera and dance companies and major symphony orchestras. On the academic side, each year several students received academic scholarships to major universities. Over 90 percent of the school's students went into post-secondary education and the graduation rate was among the highest in the state.

The school's facility was state-of-the-art. It was a beautiful building with a separate performing arts theatre. The school was a center of activity before and after school and even on the weekends. It seemed like a 24/7 school where the doors were never closed to students. It was common to see students seated at picnic tables after school with books and papers spread across the table engaged in serious conversation about a school project, an assignment, or some other discussion related to school work. The school climate of high expectations, engagement, connectedness, and support was so thick in the air that almost every student seemed to breathe it in on a daily basis. Social-emotional learning was embedded in every classroom.

My student teaching experience was in an Advanced Placement Psychology class with the best and brightest students. The supervising teacher essentially turned the class over to me three weeks into the semester. She confirmed that the students were very bright, energetic, creative high achievers. The kids were wonderfully intelligent, energetic, hard-working, inquisitive and very imaginative. They also had high expectations of their teachers, because these kids wanted and expected to learn.

After I took the measure of them and they took the measure of me, the Latin phrase *primum non nocere* (first, do no harm) came to mind, but they expected more. These students were going to learn and succeed with or without me, so my role was to be organized, encourage them to think and debate and question. I also had to intellectually challenge the students. My approach was like Greene's "stranger" concept. What does this classroom look like from the stranger's perception? Would an observer confirm that I was challenging the students at a high level, encouraging learning, and rewarding and expecting a high level of performance?

After a month in the classroom, I thought - so this is what those Level 3 classes looked like back in my high school. No wonder the kids enjoyed high school so much. In an odd way and perhaps for all of the wrong reasons, one day as I was driving home after a wonderfully rewarding experience interacting with my students I was overcome with emotion, anger really, as I thought about the wasted time and lives in my high school and in many high schools across America. Why did high school have to be such an awful experience for many students? Why is there such a disparity between public schools, between the quality of teachers and teaching and the manner in which school administrators operate schools? Why can't every school have a positive school climate and high levels of engagement? Every child should have the same education these students had, the same opportunities. If they did, perhaps some of the 7,000 students who drop out of school every day in America would instead stay in school.

Regarding dropouts, Bob Wise suggested that the following article should appear in every newspaper in America:

Washington, D.C.: Federal officials today confirmed that 7,000 teenagers vanished yesterday in broad daylight. Early reports indicate that no part of the country was spared loss; more than one-half of the missing are minority group members. 'We don't know what happened to them,' one urban official declared.

'Yesterday they were here; this afternoon, they are gone.'

I know there will never be a template for a successful public school that applies to all school settings. United States Department of Education uses standardized testing to force schools to develop templates for success. In doing so, however, the human side has not been valued. Would the United States Department of Education have mattered to me and classmates in elementary and secondary school? Would it have caused the classrooms to be more challenging for misplaced students? If it had removed the labeling and tracking; if it ensured that teachers were prepared before they begin to teach; if it had removed the draconian teachers; if it had ensured that the school was operated by a competent and caring administrative staff; if it had led to the schools offering more activities and recognition for students with more opportunities for engagement and connecting; if it had led to more positive and caring school climates; if school leadership focused as much on the nonacademic factors as the academic factors, the United States Department of Education mandates might have made a difference.

I found out that I was naïve. I did not know that the difference in language and "coding" was at the heart of public education's problems. The problem with schools is that some teachers just do not speak the same language as students or parents – literally. According to Basil Bernstein's book *Class, Codes and Control*, my problem in school, especially high school, was simply a matter of being in the wrong codebook. I suppose I had a communication class code disadvantage or disability or maybe both. Bernstein developed code theory to explain the social class differences in the communication codes of working class and middle-class children, differences that reflect the class and power relations in the social division of labor, family, and schools.

Bernstein even had empirical evidence. His work distinguished between the "restricted" code of the working class and the "elaborated" code of the middle class. Working class children and families simply did not and still do not communicate with each other or others like in the Level 3 class. Bernstein said working-class children are "restricted" while the other classes are more elaborate in their codes, more "independent and universalistic." It all has to do with the working class functioning at the production level (assembly line for nuts and bolts, for example) and the other classes functioning at the supervisory level (owns the company with assembly lines for nuts and bolts). This distinction, these different forms of language and non-verbal communications, find their way to the classroom setting.

Perhaps I misrepresent the distinguished Dr. Bernstein, but there is no doubt that the language and means and modes of communication, the code, between teachers and students vary based on the socioeconomic status on the student, or the perceived social sophistication of the student. This does not mean that all teachers who work with working class or economically disadvantaged students are not good-hearted and well-intended.

While there are teachers that are mean-spirited and elitist, there are many more who work with their students in a meaningful way, but the communication method does vary, as Bernstein says, based on the student's social class and that of the teacher. The classroom vocabulary does not garner as much attention as it should nor does the receptive and expressive language skills of students. The level of communications and the degree of expectations is dependent on the richness of the dialogue in a classroom. Assembly line talk is very different than talk in the executive suite. Talk in Advanced Placement classes is very different than talk in other classes. The talk of teachers with low expectations of students is different than the talk of teachers with high expectations of students.

Pamela Cooper's *Communication for the Classroom Teacher* acknowledges the importance of communications in the classroom and through many examples and lists of activities and strategies encourages teachers to be aware of how and what they communicate to students. She advocates the use of a wide variety of communication means, such as discussion and storytelling. The broader the range of communications, the more likely the level of interaction will move to a higher range of vocabulary and learning, and this applies to all students.

I do not have much hope that teachers will understand or adapt to the language of some kids, but that is not the point. In fact, too many teachers miss the point completely. The richness of the communication and the depth of the vocabulary that teachers use in the classroom are very important and in subtle and sometimes not so subtle ways communicate the teacher's expectation of students–high or low.

My student teaching experience included one of those cosmic transformations that we have to experience to survive in a new setting. Me, a child of the working class, now an adult, had to transform my working-class code to the social elite code of the high school where I was doing student teaching. The working-class code was somewhat tempered by my college experience, but I did not exactly replace my friends Bubba and Peggy Sue with Chip and Buffy from frat and sorority boulevard. The fact is that the college professors did not even address this issue of language and communications, despite the attention Bernstein's work claimed. Nor did they explain the dramatic effect language has on children's development and ability to learn.

Language is an essential part of our lives. It is a uniquely human element that allows us to communicate with others. Language development in large measure determines the quality of life for each of us, because the failure to develop the capacity to effectively communicate with others our wants, needs, inspirations, beliefs, knowledge, insights, feelings, motivations, intellect, fears, joys, etc. jeopardizes opportunities to experience a meaningful and productive life. The developmental trajectory of a child's language is essentially related to and connected with the child's growth socially, emotionally, and cognitively. Language connects the senses, stimulates the mind, promotes logic, provides the means for understanding and projecting images, and informs the development of self as well as moral development and self-regulation and social competency.

Noam Chomsky said that language mirrors human mental processes and shapes the flow and character of thought. The philosopher John Stuart Mill said, *"Language is the light of the mind"* – the representation of a fundamental expression of social identity.

With the evidence linking children's language with behavior, social interactions, and other developmental skills, why has this information not been more widely reported and used? Part of the issue if not the primary issue is the oversimplification of language itself. Most people, including professionals, underestimate the complexity of language; therefore, they dismiss or overlook the determinants that impact language development. Even though it seems simple to produce and understand language, it is very complex. According to Snow, *"We have to be able to access our lexicon—our mental store of words and organize these into meaningful sentences that convey our ideas."* A person has to learn the relationship between and among language structure, pragmatics, and use.

The structure of language is further complicated by the medium of transmission, including phonics, phonology, and grammar that requires an understanding of morphology (linguistics to understand the form of words) and syntax (arrangement of words and phrases to create meaningful sentences). Language structure also includes semantical understanding (meaning of words), lexicon parlance and discourse. Discourse refers to the unit of language that is longer than one sentence and is often more broadly used in both the written and spoken social context. If there is a deficit in any of these elements of language's complex architecture, a child's ability to effectively use language can be compromised.

While the research shows a link between children's language deficits and their development, what precisely are language deficits and how are they manifest in the developmental stages of children? Language problems include impairment in expressive and/or receptive language development; deficits in indirect communications skills (such as comprehending indirect instructions); pragmatic deficits (including non-verbal expression and understanding), and deficits in language processing – interpretation, meaning, and response. Language deficits also include the inability to process and understand everyday abstract language, including the idioms, sarcasm, and metaphors that are used to enliven typical communications and dramatize or emphasize critically important communications. Children with language deficits experience considerable confusion with social context expressions such as, *"The homework is a breeze;"* or *"Nothing is written in stone."* Children without adequately developed language skills typically understand communications at the basic levels, so they do not comprehend anything beyond the concrete level – what they hear is taken literally because the language deficits do not allow them to decipher abstract forms of expression or communications.

Understanding the complexity of language goes beyond its architecture. To more fully understand the architecture of language, it is also important to identify the determinants that impact the development of the various components of language. Research by the Early Intervention Foundation called "Language as a Child Wellbeing Indicator" described how the architecture of language becomes the growth of language. The two major components of language growth are expressive language and receptive language. Expressive language includes speech, gestures, and outward communications while receptive language is concisely described as understanding others. Graphically, the Foundation researchers depict the growth of language as a tree. The metaphor has expressive language described as the part of the tree that is visible above ground and receptive language is described as below ground or the roots of language that are based on comprehension which is not so readily apparent to observers. The "tree of language" cannot thrive or even exist without the "roots of comprehension." According to the researchers,

Comprehension, or receptive language, is the root, underpinning all expressive language. When children understand what others are saying, they are more likely to be able to use those expressions themselves.

Continuing the tree metaphor, the trunk depicts vocabulary which is essential to growing healthy and strong before the branches of grammar and morphology can thrive to produce the leaves of speech sounds. The illustrative and functionally descriptive metaphor also notes the impact of the "air of social context" on language. This refers to the skill in language that allows children to understand the context in which language is communicated. For example, we know that when the teacher says "*Man, it is cold in here, the window is open*" she probably means "*Could you go and close it please?*" But the child must infer that this is what is intended. An understanding of context is also necessary for children to master the figurative use of various language elements, such as with jokes, metaphors, and idioms. Without this, common expressions such as "*raining cats and dogs*" would be taken literally – and very incorrectly.

Teacher preparation programs typically give scant attention to language and communication skills in the classroom in a meaningful way. Recently at a conference round-table discussion, a university professor said, "*It doesn't really matter what we teach in college or train teachers what to do in college, because when they step into the public classroom the culture of the school takes over.*" That is not entirely accurate. Teacher preparation programs need to change and change quickly; they are not preparing teachers for the classroom. Likewise, school districts need to change. If there is not a focus on improving school climate, new teachers have very little chance of succeeding and staying and veteran teachers will look elsewhere, too, or simply try to survive.

CHAPTER 17
WATERLINES AND GRADUATE SCHOOL

Sometimes I lie awake at night, and ask, 'Where have I gone wrong?' Then a voice says to me, 'This is going to take more than one night.'

-Charlie Brown

I visited my college job placement and career counselor. She showed me a list of potential jobs, none of which paid any more than the blue-collar job I had at the county water department. She said great wealth was within my grasp if only I would get a graduate degree in psychology. She showed me job openings for master level psychology graduates. In just two years in the School of Clinical Psychology, I could emerge with a college degree that might have job market value. I was hooked. I liked psychology a great deal and this was a career within my grasp that I might enjoy.

I applied for the School of Clinical Psychology and was accepted. There was one small problem. I was told that the program was so rigorous and demanding that I could not have a job; I had to be a full-time student. I told the Dean of the Clinical Psychology program that I made it through four years of college working full-time and I was certain I could continue that pace without much trouble. *"Oh, no,"* he said, *"you don't understand how rough this program can be for students – they have to go to classes, go to labs, and write research papers."* What the hell did he think I had been doing for the last four years, plus working 40 hours per week? It was obvious that to become a clinical psychologist so I could learn how to work with people about life's issues I had to first remove myself from life. I further explained to the good Dean that I lived alone and I had to pay rent, pay bills, and eat. He was unmoved. I then asked if I might qualify as a graduate school assistant so that I would have at least enough money to continue my subterranean apartment living and soup life. He said no to that, also. I had not applied soon enough; I had not visited the clinical psychology school while in undergraduate school, and I did not talk like he did. I was speaking the wrong code.

Meantime, back in the water meter box world, the back-breaking work routine continued uninterrupted until one day I saw a huge man dressed in an ill-fitting sports coat with a crew cut straight out of the Marine Corp manual, and a purposeful walk heading toward me. He was a big man with a voice so deep it sounded like thunder. He was the director of the county water department and he visited me one winter afternoon shortly after I started my nightly chore of loading the cast iron meter boxes unto the trucks. He stood in the parking lot wearing a well-worn sports coat, rumpled dingy white shirt, thin tie, and pants too short for his height and smoking a cigar. I stopped for a moment, waiting for him to beckon me and to shout out something to me over the noise of the large truck engines. Instead, he motioned with a hand gesture that clearly meant "*get back to work.*" I stepped up the pace. After standing there watching me for about thirty minutes, he approached me. A man of few words, he asked, "*Did you take mechanical drawing in high school?*" I may not be the brightest guy in the world, but I figured this guy must have something in mind that just might be better than loading heavy cast iron meter boxes, so I said, *"Yes, sir – tops in my class in high school mechanical drawing."* I did not take mechanical drawing in high school, but I did walk past the class a few times. *"Good,"* he said, *"I have a project for you."*

The next afternoon, instead of reporting to the cast iron hell-hole I showed up as instructed at the main office of the county water department, which was housed in a depression era CCA building. My new job was to trace old water lines from fading and torn 12 x 16 pages onto new pages. There were stacks upon stacks of these huge dust-covered books filled with roughly and crudely drawn diagrams of streets and water lines and shut off valves dating back to the 1940s and 1950s. There was a drawing of every street in the county. The county is 271 square miles. That's a lot of roads, water lines, water shut off valves, and fire hydrants. My boss simply said, *"Update these damn drawings so we can read the damn things, cause when we send a damn crew out to repair a damn water line break they can't find the damn water shut off valves or even the damn waterline sometimes cause these damn drawings are either hard to read or are not accurate – damn drawings."* Seems to me that you just go to where the water puddle is and follow the leak, but I just nodded my head thoughtfully to convey understanding and sympathy. I was not about to argue with a big, angry guy who managed to use the word "damn" eight times in one sentence in one breath.

What I got out of the deal was an indoor job with plenty of heating and air conditioning, no raw and bleeding hands, no back-breaking work, and more money. The hours were the same, 4:00 p.m. to midnight.

In my new job, each afternoon and well into the night I spread the old drawings on a lighted table (a table with a light underneath) and literally trace the drawings onto a clean piece of paper. Simple enough except many times the old drawing was so faded I could not read them. And if I could not pinpoint where the water lines were supposed to be on a street based on the old drawing, I had to physically go to that street with a water line detector and a sketch pad before dark. Using a water line detector is less science and more voodoo. I would have done just as well with a forked stick. Sometimes the old drawings showed the water line on the wrong side of the road. It took me a while to figure that one out, but after no readings on the sophisticated water line detection device and trembling water finder forked stick, it occurred to me that the drawings were not accurate. Sometimes I wondered around streets, yards, sidewalks, etc. trying to find the water line.

Water line shut off valves are supposed to be clearly marked above ground with a small circular metal cover, but that was not always the case. In fact, I must admit that after wondering for hours looking for these valves, I would decide that my guess was as good as anybody's so I drew where I thought the water valve should be based primarily on the nearest fire hydrant.

For the most part, I was now indoors most of my afternoons and evenings, alone in a very large old building. It was wonderful. I could do my drawings, tracings, and study during my meal break. The measure of my performance was the number of tracings I left on the boss's desk at night. He was usually gone from the building by the time I arrived, so we communicated by notes. His notes typically were something along the lines of "Ok." He was not a talkative person. My notes were similar, such as *"Ten minutes late, took a short meal break, in early tomorrow."* Or, *"I can't find the water line so I'm making this stuff up as I go along."* Only in my dreams would I write that one.

I still had to clock in and clock out, but sometimes I would clock out and remain in the building to study. There were distractions and temptations on the way home from work and even in my apartment complex while the large old building was quiet, the lighting was good, it was comfortable, and I had ample space. It was like a library – a great place to study. Plus, the building had a huge vending machine and everything in it was only a dime.

Once I got the hang of mechanical drawing, I could generate several drawings each night. My boss seemed pleased with the work and I had all manner of time to spend in the old building studying. It would be much more interesting to read if I had brought women or drugs into the building, but I need neither. Instead, I brought books and other study materials into the building.

I did not give up on the idea of attending graduate school even though the clinical psychology snobs derailed me. I enjoyed learning and I enjoyed college very much. Since the clinical psychology program did not want people like me who had to work for a living, I looked for other possible graduate studies. Community counseling sounded interesting until I learned that there was no demand for anyone with that degree. The thought of school counseling made me shutter. I could not picture myself working with students like me.

I was in the career counseling center at the university one day, when a professor happened by as I was looking at the job posting bulletin board. He said, *"Are you looking for a graduate program or a job?"* I said, *"Preferably a graduate program that will lead to a job."* *"Step right up, young man, I have the perfect career for you,"* he said, or something like that.

Just the experience of being somewhat recruited was intoxicating. The chair of the Department of School Psychology showed me to his office. It was a very impressive sight. It was a comfortable size and filled with awards and degrees hanging all over the place. He had an Oriental rug, expensive furniture, and nice paintings. There were photographs of him with rich and famous people. This was obviously a professor of influence and means. He had his peculiarities like most professors who are removed from the world of real work, but he was charming, enthusiastic, intelligent and sincere. He introduced me to the idea of applying for graduate school in the field of school psychology.

What is school psychology? The frequently used definition comes from the National Association of School Psychologists:

School psychologists are highly trained in both psychology and education. They must complete a minimum of a Specialist-level degree program (60 graduate semester credits) that includes a 1200-hour internship and emphasizes preparation in the following: data-based decision making, consultation and collaboration, effective instruction, child development, student diversity and development, school organization, prevention, intervention, mental health, learning styles, behavior, research, and program evaluation. School psychologists must be certified and/or licensed by the state in which they work.

I thought school psychology was a new field, but the professor informed me that the Division of School Psychology was added to the American Psychological Association in 1945. However, the National Association of School Psychologists (NASP) was not formed until 1969.

The job market for school psychologists was on the edge of booming when the professor talked me into applying for the school psychology graduate program. The federal Education of All Handicapped Children Act (EHA) required states to provide free and appropriate public education to all children between the ages of 3 to 21. This act required all children to attend school, including children who previously might not have received public education due to their physical, emotional, or intellectual disabilities. EHA mandated children be educated in the "least restricted environment" appropriate for them (in regular education classrooms when possible), and they must be re-evaluated at least every three years by a school psychologist.

Due in large part to the EHA Act, the profession of school psychology flourished as the students needed additional support to be successful in the regular school setting and because of the focus on individual student testing, retesting, and consultation. No other field offered the combination of psychology and education like school psychology, so school districts across the nation started posting positions for school psychologists. However, most of the school districts were hiring only a few school psychologists. Small school districts typically hired only one school psychologist or shared one school psychologist with other school districts.

I told the professor that it all sounded promising, but I had to work while attending graduate school. He said that was not a problem. I could pursue a career in school psychology and work full-time. I could do this. I could live modestly while attending graduate school - continue living in the cheap apartment, continue tracing water lines, continue searching for water valves, continue living on 25 cent hamburgers and 10 cent candies. *"All that stands between the graduate and the top of the ladder is the ladder."* (Anonymous)

When I started graduate school, I felt like the ladder reached through the clouds. I could not see the end anywhere in sight. When I was in the comfortable confines of the professor's office, two years to complete the degree program did not seem that far away, but when I saw 60 graduate hours on paper and when I saw the list of graduate classes laid out before me, I realized had difficult the journey would be and maybe I was biting off more than I could chew.

I had to laugh to myself and at myself for that attitude because I was not that far removed from those awful days contemplating the bleak prospects of my future while standing in front of a water vat with both arms below sea level trying to cool off the scalding hot plastic. It is good to keep life in perspective.

I was accepted into the school psychology graduate program at the university. The summer before I started my graduate career, I had surgery on one of my ankles, so on my first day of graduate school, I was trying to negotiate a stick shift car with my right foot in a cast. This was followed by scary efforts on crutches negotiating around downtown streets, sidewalks, and construction. With the congestion on the streets, pedestrians do not wait for crossing lights. They just slip between the cars that are gridlocked and dance between the lanes. Most of the sidewalks were leaning drastically to the right or left, were under construction, or obstructed by some other urban obstacle. It was safer to just walk in the street. One does not notice all of this except on two occasions – the first time visit to the city and when you're on crutches.

I stumbled, slipped, danced, and dodged my way to class. I was running late that first day. Great, I am going to be late for my first graduate class, I thought, when I tripped over yet another gap in the sidewalk. As I approached the classroom, I was trying to be cool, because a graduate student must be at least two degrees cooler than an undergraduate student. Instead, I practically fell into the classroom when one crutch caught on the door frame. It is very difficult to look cool when hopping on one foot while one crutch is sliding across the classroom floor and the other crutch is standing alone hugging the doorframe as if waiting to be asked to enter the room. The most uncool part was that the doorframe-hugging crutch was cooler than me. The small gathering of students was trying mightily to keep a straight face while the professor was sitting on a small stool, the picture of coolness just waiting for me to end the show. The professor was a handsome, debonair man wearing a mock turtleneck and a sports coat. He was at least three degrees cooler than any other professor at the university. He had Hollywood idol looks and a James Earl Jones voice. More importantly, he was both smart and intelligent and he had a great sense of humor. He had seen many sides of life and was smart in a worldly, perceptive way and he was very intelligent in the academic sense. He liked to laugh, and he liked for his students to question concepts, research, opinions, everything. He encouraged debate and dialog. He wanted students who were creative thinkers.

The professor was fresh from the University of California at Berkeley, where he was one of the first Black students to earn a Ph.D. in educational psychology/school psychology. Even though he had taught classes at Berkeley, the professorship at my university was his first as a full-time professor. In fact, the day I stumbled into his class was his first class at the university. So, not only did I make a clumsy impression for myself, I am certain I cast doubt in his mind about students from Georgia, the Southeast, and all regions east of the Mississippi. For many years after that day, he reminded me of our first class together.

CHAPTER 18
MTSS

No psychologist should pretend to understand what he does not understand. Only fools and charlatans know everything and understand nothing.

–Anton Chekhov

For many school psychologists, it seems that their primary job duty is to evaluate students for placement in special education classes. While this attitude and expectation has changed in some school districts, there is still the belief that the school psychologist's role is primarily that of test administrator for special education.

There is a reason to be hopeful that this component of public education will change. The national move toward Multi-tiered Systems of Support (MTSS), if applied appropriately, has and will continue to reduce the reliance on psychometric tests to find reasons and solutions for student academic and/or behavioral problems in schools, and will reduce the number of students referred to special education.

With MTSS, schools identify students at risk for poor learning outcomes, monitor student progress, provide evidence-based interventions and adjust the intensity and nature of those interventions depending on a student's responsiveness.

MTSS is a tiered delivery model: (1) Standards-Based classroom learning (all students participate in general education that includes universal screenings to target students in need of specific instructional support, teachers provide instruction that allows for different learning styles, and student learning is monitored by formative assessments); (2) Needs-Based (in addition to Tier 1, students who have difficulty are identified and strategies are established to address the student's needs – with ample implementation time); (3) Student Support (a more concentrated and precise effort to address the needs of students, again with specific strategies and time for implementation) and specially designed (this can include special education).

MTSS is one of those rare things in public education. It is a strategy with sound research, sound reasoning, a sound purpose, can be implemented without a budget burden, has sustainability, it makes sense, and it gives students a chance to mature and respond to low levels of support before being identified as a special education student.

Because of MTSS, some states and many school districts have seen the number of students being referred to special education classes decline. In many school districts, fewer students are being referred to special education classes and more students are leaving special education classes. Public education should make a more concentrated effort to train all educators about MTSS, and more school districts should be encouraged to implement MTSS in its purest form.

In Georgia, the state legislature passed a bill in 2018 that restricts the suspension and expulsion of preschool through third-grade students. The young students may not be suspended for more than five days without first being referred to MTSS (with the caveat that the restriction does not apply to serious violations such as weapons and drugs).

Special education classes are the salvation of many students, but over the years too many students have been labeled special education that in fact just needed some extra help, encouragement, needed a little extra time to mature both intellectually and physically, were hampered by a negative school climate and/or a negative classroom climate, or had an undiagnosed physical problem. For that reason, psychological testing, particularly with children, should be approached in a very cautious way, and parents of children who are evaluated should be encouraged to ask questions, especially questions about MTSS.

One of the first schools I was assigned to when I became a full-time school psychologist was one of those schools built during the open classroom era, which was an educational fad backed by no research. The schools were considered "open" because there were no walls to separate classes. The concept caused chaos and was a dismal failure.

The open classroom concept caused collateral damage. I received a referral on a third-grade student who refused to come to school. Everyone, including his therapist and the student's mother, was quick to diagnose the student as "school phobic." They wanted to use behavior modification to bring him around. His therapist even considered medication. Since the student would not come to school, I went to his house with a social worker.

The home was a modest middle-class home nicely furnished and expertly maintained in a typical suburban community. The young boy was small for his age but smart and articulate. He said he was never going back to the school because *"No one cares if I'm at school or not and because it's so noisy there!"* I asked if he liked the first and second grades and he only shrugged and said yes they were okay. But he seldom missed a day of school in K-2 grades. I decided that this student benefitted from and needed structure and a school day schedule. He would not ride to school with his mother, older brother, or on the school bus. One morning after visiting with him at his home, he agreed to ride to school with me. This was the first time he mentioned going to school in a week. He'd even told the juvenile court social worker that he wasn't going back to school and the judge could lock him up. So, when he suddenly announced that morning that he wanted to ride to school with me it was a shock. On the way to school, he said he wanted to see if the classrooms were "still chaotic." When we arrived at the school, the principal was near the front day and made a grand gesture to welcome the little boy. That tough veneer was broken, and the little boy was escorted to the "partially open classroom" by the principal.

The teachers with the thankful permission of the principal divided the classrooms with tall bookshelves—they created their own classroom walls and the students responded very positively. The bookshelf-divided classrooms had regained their order and the classrooms were functioning more normally. The little boy who was so negatively impacted by the open classroom settled into a routine and maintained good attendance the rest of the year.

The principal told me later that he wondered how many children were blamed for misbehavior or poor attendance when in fact it was the school's fault for chasing an education fad. That's an example of how the MTSS process is essential. The MTSS team considers all possibilities of reasons for the student's problems. It may be a physical problem (e.g., 25% percent of students have vision problems that are correctable, but many cannot afford glasses), response to trauma from home, a learning disability, the classroom climate (or the configuration of the classroom) or the school climate. Educators must become more adept at being problem solvers instead of looking for remedies that are short-term and fall short of being a solution. Providing a remedy, like out-of-school suspension, does not address the basic problem; it only addresses the presenting problem. When providing a remedy, the problem will almost always come back. It takes time to find a solution, but our children deserve that of us.

CHAPTER 19
BOY'S LIFE

Children are like wet cement. Whatever falls on them makes an impression.

-Haim Ginott

There is no way to know for certain because educators and researcher do not keep such records, but it is logical to assert that millions of dollars and thousands of hours of instructional time were wasted on public education's open classroom fad that had no basis in research. The concept sounded good and certainly, the best-selling books that advocated it as a way to ensure that America would produce happy and successful citizens could not be wrong, as obviously many people thought.

The larger issue in the 1970s and 1980s was the growing belief that public education was a mess and that public education was the means to address any and all of the ills of society that were supposedly caused by public education and at the same time and perhaps for the same reasons public education became in many ways vulnerable to the latest fad or social experimentation.

If education is the antidote for increasing youth crime; if "unwarranted" suspensions and expulsions were adding to the problem; if more and more students were being placed in special education classes; if housing patterns were creating more and larger and impersonal suburban schools; if integration was still struggling to be a part of the social fabric; if criticism of public schools was persistent; if fads like the open classroom did not work, then what exactly would and should public education look like in the future?

The future included the world, even though many people including educators where blinded by the egocentric notion that the United States was and would continue to be the center of the universe.

In addition to the changes already mentioned, the world came knocking on public education's door unlike before. The amendment to the *Bilingual Education Act* (BEA) was passed and the amendment was more significant than most people know now or perceived at that time. According to the National Clearinghouse on Bilingual Education, the Act defined a bilingual education program as one that provided instruction in English and in the native language of the student to allow the student to progress effectively through the educational system.

English as a second language (ESL) programs alone were considered insufficient. The goal of a bilingual program was to prepare students to participate effectively in the regular classroom as quickly as possible. However, maintaining the native language and culture of the students was not excluded.

The BEA Act mandated the establishment of regional support centers of consultants and trainers to provide guidance and support to schools. A national clearinghouse for bilingual education was also mandated to collect and disseminate information to school districts supporting programs and identifying resources. Finally, the BEA Act mandated capacity-building efforts. The federal government would fund school districts' major new efforts to expand curricula, staff, and research for bilingual programs as part of an effort to expand services to bilingual students. This was to enable the school districts to develop enough expertise to operate bilingual education programs without federal assistance (after such programs had been established and implemented).

The world had arrived at the door of public education in the United States. The message was growing very clear that all educators better be thinking of how to change education to fit the new world and meet the needs of all students. The old way of operating schools would have to change. Buckminster Fuller said, *"Don't fight to change the existing system; create a new system that makes the current system obsolete."*

While the world of public education was beginning to change at a break-neck pace, I was concerned about passing my internship, paying college tuition, keeping my water department job, paying the rent, and keeping a little food on the table. The monthly fee for a basement apartment, plus tuition, books, gas, food, etc. did not exactly match my monthly wages from the water department. My life was simple in theory and stressful in practice – go to school, go to work, go home and study, eat and sleep and then do it all over again.

My school psychology internship was an interesting experience. I was in a public school at least three days each week working with students under the supervision of a certified school psychologist. The students were great to work with even though they had a variety of issues.

One tiny elementary age girl had a terrible, uncontrollable temper. Even the boys were afraid of her when she lost her temper. She would go into a wild, screaming and aggressive rage. After the screaming rage, she would be just as sweet as a little girl could be. It did not take Sigmund Freud to discover the genesis of her behavior after meeting with her parents. This only child ruled the house – totally and completely. She was a bright girl with good social skills, but it was difficult to ignore her head-spinning, screaming, bile-spitting episodes. She is the type of child that can ruin dinner for everyone in a restaurant because of her loud outbursts. I think the parents of the little girl were concerned that a demon spirit had moved into their quiet neighborhood and had taken up residence in their daughter.

My supervisor and I reassured them that it was not a demon spirit causing their little girl to act like a demon-possessed miniature witch. It was the result of crummy parenting on their part. Of course, we did not use those terms. I think they were hoping that an exorcism would do the trick instead of the more challenging solution of being a responsible parent with the capacity to say "no" and mean it. We had a lot of work to do with the parents. To the parents, the weekly parenting classes were a revelation. They slowly but certainly embraced the notion that the truest expression of love and concern for children requires teaching them discipline. Children want their parents to be their parents, not their friends. Over time, the little girl's tantrums diminished significantly as the parents took control of the house and her behavior.

I evaluated typical students and students with learning and other disabilities. I learned that a school psychologist can jump right into an evaluation and be coldly efficient about it, or a school psychologist can take a few minutes to help a student relax and even enjoy the individual attention during an evaluation. It is imperative for a school psychologist to do the latter. The whole idea of an evaluation is to get a true picture, as much as possible, of the student's strengths, weaknesses, potential, and what makes the student tick, which is less likely to be accomplished if the student is terrified during the evaluation process.

Another student I worked with was an 11–year-old boy who was large for his age and kept a perpetual snarl. He was struggling academically, always had, and he was the classroom bully with an aggressive attitude toward everyone, including the teachers.

When we met, he wanted nothing to do with being evaluated. That opinion did not come from any insight on my part. It seemed obvious when he said, *"What's this crap you want me to do?" "This is kid's stuff." "I ain't doing none of this."*

Fortunately, what I wanted to do and what I did were two very different approaches to working with this difficult student. I will skip over what I wanted to do and go straight to what I did. I displayed a great deal of patience, and I skipped around for some topic that the student had an interest in before beginning the testing session formally. I did a lot of topic exploration before I hit on anything that he had an interest in. Oddly enough, he liked to read *Boy's Life* magazine. In fact, he was enamored with *Boy's Life* magazine, which is a general interest magazine published monthly in editions for boys from first grade through high school. *Boy's Life* is the flagship youth publication of the Boy Scouts of America. Many stories and articles in *Boy's Life* reflect the program themes of Cub Scouting and program features of Boy Scouting. It includes stories, photos, pictures, puzzles, jokes, news, etc. Almost every pediatrician's office and dentist's office in America has copies of *Boy's Life* magazine in their waiting rooms or once did. If I were a kid, I would have grave misgivings about a doctor or dentist who did not have copies of *Boy's Life* in the waiting area. The absence of *Boy's Life* magazine in a doctor's waiting room was a clear indication that the doctor did not like children.

What was odd about the student's fascination with *Boy's Life* is that he was not a good reader, according to the teacher and the evaluation referral form, and he did not seem to enjoy reading of any type in class. What was equally odd was how I found out about his enjoyment of reading *Boy's Life*.

In my effort to get him to relax and perhaps trust me a little bit, I spent some time trying to find out more about his day-to-day routine at school and home. I asked simple, straight-forward questions like *"What do you like to do?"* I received many grunts and inarticulate, unintelligible, and grumpy responses.

Finally, in desperation to find something to talk about I asked about the band-aid on his forearm. He said he got his arm caught on a piece of barbed wire and it cut him. I took off on a series of questions about his injury and his visit to the doctor's office. He said he had to wait a long time for the doctor. I made a comment like *"I bet that drove you crazy waiting in the doctor's office."* He said, *"No, I didn't mind because I like reading Boy's Life and that's the only place they have that magazine."* When I asked him about the magazine, his eyes lit up and he described the stories, puzzles, and jokes as his favorite sections. He seemed genuinely surprised when I told him that his school library had *Boy's Life*. He did not believe me, so we went to the school's library. I told him he could read it while I did some paperwork. I discretely watched him while he read *Boy's Life*. He could read and he could concentrate, and the snarl was not perpetual after all. We had some discussion about the contents of the magazine which gave me the chance to ease into the evaluation.

I will not say he enjoyed the evaluation overall, but he did willingly participate. We were able to identify areas of academic weakness as well as some strengths. I shared some remediation ideas with teachers, and he became part of a small counseling group that met with the school counselor. The motivation for his participation was good behavior and a chance to go to the library and read *Boy's Life* magazine. Occasionally his classroom teacher gave him the opportunity to discuss topics from *Boy's Life* in class.

Who would have guessed or ever discovered what a simple and fulfilling joy this young kid found in reading *Boy's Life*? It was a scary experience for me to realize how fragile children are and how easy it is to miss opportunities to help them. I completely stumbled onto something that seemed insignificant but what turned out to be very important in his life. It would have been so easy to miss that. It would have been so easy to write a report that included references about his anger and his reluctance to cooperate with the examiner. He could have been on the path to an Emotional-Behavioral Disorder diagnosis or facing chronic suspensions as he grew older. As he learned to deal with this anger and frustration, he quit bullying the other students and became a participatory student.

CHAPTER 20
GNATS OR METRO

Life is what happens to you while you're busy making other plans.

-John Lennon

In the 1980s, there were not very many job openings for school psychologists because of the sudden economic downturn. The downward trend was not because the need wasn't there, it was primarily because school systems were struggling with their budgets.

The field of school psychology was emerging at that time and would move from professional step-child status to recognition and acceptance by the American Psychological Association. Soon thereafter school districts across the nation started hiring school psychologists but some were waiting for more clear signs that the economy would not slip into a recession before filling open positions.

In the meantime, I was losing my taste for life in the basement apartment, life at the water department, life with water on my cereal instead of milk, and McDonald hamburgers. Fortunately, the overwhelming need for a lifestyle change coincided with the completion of my graduate work. I earned a master's degree in school psychology and became a state certified school psychologist. Upon graduation, I had one job opportunity-only one. All of that work and yet I had only one offer.

There is an area of Georgia referred to as the "Gnat Line," which essentially is any part of Georgia south of middle Georgia. Gnats especially love the southern-most part of Georgia, where it is ungodly hot and humid from May to September. Gnats are annoying flying insects that are about the size of a pinhead and they live for the sole purpose to swarm around the ears, eyes, nose, and mouth of mammals in order to drive them to the brink of insanity. They can drive an otherwise healthy and normal human being to speak in tongues. The one job opportunity I had was well below the Gnat Line, in a very rural southwest corner of Georgia.

On a very hot day in early June, I drove to a cinder block building south of Albany, Georgia to meet with Regional Education Service Agency (RESA) staff members to interview for a job. RESA is a cooperative funded by the state to provide training and other services for regions across the state. RESAs are vital to small, rural school districts that do not have money for staff training. If I was hired and accepted the position, I would have been the lone school psychologist for five small school districts.

The school districts were in counties with open fields, wetlands, farmland, dirt roads, creeks, rivers, streams, pine forests, pecan groves, cotton fields, soybean fields, peanut fields, and cattle. My only experience with public education at that time had been in a large metropolitan and suburban area, so I was in for a rude awakening.

The main office of the RESA was a tiny circa 1940's cinder block building nestled among beautiful huge oak trees. The parking lot was sand and gravel. My shirt was already damp from my car air conditioner's losing battle with the heat and humidity, and it did not improve when I went inside the building.

I was greeted in the kindest and most respectful manner by the secretary. I don't know how she maintained such a positive attitude in such a rundown and hot building. The conditioned air came from a window unit that was struggling to push out any coolness. Nevertheless, the secretary was gracious, smiling, and each member of the interview team shared the same courteous and grateful attitude. After a few questions, they told me about the job, about the travel and about the schools and the communities. There would be extensive travel between schools, and there would be limited community resources. The closest hospital was in Albany, almost an hour's drive away. There were no mental health counselors or psychologists any closer than that, and only one physician in the area. Housing was a challenge, also. To let an apartment, I would have to look toward the Albany area, which was an hour one way. Rental homes were not available in the area either. I did not mind the travel between schools so much, but to drive almost an hour just to get to the area and then drive several more miles to the schools was not an attractive prospect. I guess those thoughts were revealed unintentionally by my facial expression because the interview team said that they would pay for the gas and they would help me find an apartment or rental house. They were kind and sweet-natured people. They made me feel important and needed.

Even though the school year ended the week before, I wanted to visit a couple of the schools to get a feel for the area and the schools. We drove for several miles before we came to an elementary school. The school was on flat land surrounded on three sides with heavy woods and a section of wetlands. The palmettos and summer flowers such as

~235~

Bachelor's Button, Black-eyed Susan, Cardinal Flowers, Coreopsis, Purple Coneflowers, and others flowers around the school were beautifully maintained and the grass was trimmed almost flat to the ground. The parking lot was sand and gravel that was perfectly manicured. The school was built in 1952 in the E shape with a flat roof. It was all brick and one level. There was no central air conditioning, but each room had a window air conditioning unit.

The principal, a hefty, jolly man in his fifties greeted me kindly. This was the first thing he said after introductions, "*We hope to get central A.C. installed within a couple of years.*" He then described the students, families, and his faculty. He told a story of a close-knit community with few resources but a willingness to help each other. There was great respect for the teachers but it was a challenge to recruit and keep teachers. Despite the challenges, the principal was proud of his school, his community, and his staff.

It was obvious that the principal and the custodial staff and other staff members took pride in the school and how it was maintained, and they had a wonderful relationship with the community. At least twice each year, the community would help clean the building and grounds. The principal would cook BBQ and hot dogs for the volunteers.

They were doing the best with what little they had, but the facility was not on par with what the students and staff members deserved and needed. The media center was painfully bare of books and other media resources, as were the classrooms, and there was very little technology for students or teachers. The school system simply did not have the funding to do more than they were doing.

While I was disappointed with the resources and less than enthusiastic about the prospects of housing problems and travel requirements, I was very impressed with the attitude of everyone I talked to. Everyone talked about the students with sincere concern; they knew the families well; they knew the needs of students, parents, and staff; and they knew that somehow, some way, things needed to change.

During the long drive back to Atlanta, I was flooded with thoughts of the schools I visited and the very nice people I had spent the day with. I was trying to balance all of the factors – logically, it made more sense to remain in the metro area until a job became available, which I knew one would because 40 percent of Georgia's public school students live in the metro-Atlanta area. But those thoughts conflicted with my heart. I felt welcomed and needed there in South Georgia. For the first time, I knew I had something to offer to others that could be very useful. I could help those students and that community. I was very conflicted, but at the time it seemed to be my destiny, and as long as I did not have to live in a basement apartment and eat Cornflakes at every meal, southwest Georgia was fine with me. Bring on the gnats.

Just as I was about to accept the offer in southwest Georgia, I received a call from the school system in the metropolitan area where I attended school. Yes, the same school district that reluctantly claimed me as a student years earlier, and the same community where the juvenile judge would probably still remember my name. While I was reluctant for many reasons, it was a job near home and the pay was substantially more than in rural Georgia.

There was one catch about the job opening: they were not completely certain the position was going to be open, but they would know within 72 hours. In the meantime, they wanted me to come in for an interview. I now had one firm job offer and one possible job offer. I did have a dilemma, however. The one firm job offer did not pay as much as the one possible job offer and it was in a rural area of Georgia that is not conducive to social life and would greatly reduce the chances of more graduate education. However, in all fairness to the nice people, I could not keep southwest Georgia waiting, so I told my former school district I needed to know within 48 hours about the position. I had for the most part given up on the metropolitan job when in the 46th hour I was offered a job as a school psychologist. I was glad to stay in the area, but I was not too excited about working for my old school district, and that telephone call to the good folks in southwest Georgia was very difficult. It is thought-provoking to think about how very different my life would be working in rural school districts instead of an urban area.

Typically, school psychologists are assigned to a cluster of schools. As a new inexperienced employee I was assigned to work in 12 schools, all except one was predominantly Black. The one school that was predominantly white would change in less than two years to a predominantly black student population due to rapidly changing demographics and white flight. At that time, the predominantly black schools were in the southern part of the county and the predominantly white schools were in the central and northern section of the county.

All of this was irrelevant to me at the time and I was oblivious to this. I was just delighted to have a job. However, system-wide practices created several serious issues later.

CHAPTER 21
FROM LEADERLESS TO SERVANT LEADER

The schools ain't what they used to be and never was.

−Will Rogers

My first day on the job was spent driving to each of the 12 schools to introduce myself to the principals. If people want a quick fix to many of the problems in public education, it can start in the principal's office.

One principal refused to see me. I did not take it personally, because he refused to see everybody. The man would get to the elementary school early before anyone else arrived, and he would remain in his office with the door closed for most of the day. No sounds, either intentional or otherwise, were ever heard coming from behind his door. His lunch was brought to his door by the secretary. She knocked on the door and he opened the door just wide enough to gather in his lunch tray. I was surprised she did not just slip it under his door. He rarely attended his own faculty meetings and he seldom attended PTA meetings. Complaints from teachers and parents to the central office did not change the principal's total lack of involvement in the school nor did the central office respond to the complaints. The school, which was located in a very economically poor neighborhood, was dirty, the classrooms disorderly, the teachers demoralized, and the parents were not welcomed in the school. It was the worst school climate I've ever experienced. Most of the teachers were first or second-year teachers whose sole purpose in life at that time was to get transferred to another school, preferably a school in the north section of the county where the schools were cleaner. I learned very early that if you can smell the odors from the restrooms as soon as you walk into a school from any outside door the chances are almost 100 percent that it is a poorly run school with a negative school climate. This was one of those schools. Over 30 years later, I still see a relationship between the cleanliness of a school, school climate, and school effectiveness. If parents want a snapshot of a school's climate, base it on the smell of the school. If the dominating smell is urine, it's probably not the best school for their children.

Some schools may overcome the principal's indifference if they have a strong, caring dynamic assistant principal. This school was not that fortunate. The assistant principal was running a real estate business out of her office and had very little time for the school. Since I could not work with the phantom principal and because the school counselor was swamped with student and parent issues, the assistant principal was my contact person at the school. When I went to school I would go to her disheveled office. Her window curtains hung at an odd angle because they were barely hanging at all. She had stacks of papers in every corner of the office. Paper wrappers from fast-food restaurants littered her office and provided proof that she seldom ventured into the school cafeteria. She had a planter that contained either an emaciated dead plant from the previous century or the remains of a kid who got lost trying to find the door to escape from her office. The office smelled like a combination of Vicks Vapor, mustard, and cough syrup. That is probably what she put on her hamburgers. In her stumbling, bumbling manner of moving about her office, she would give me a stack of referrals from teachers of students they thought should be tested. She had the very annoying habit, well there were many, but the most annoying was her inability to make complete sentences when describing students: "*Johnny is so strange, well and you know Mae is really kind of strange, and of course Billy in a strange way is kind of well, and he ....*" After working with her it was easy to see why the word strange was near and dear to her.

Many of the reasons for the testing referrals were because a teacher thought certain students should be placed into special education classes. It was sad but true that ill-prepared teachers, black or white, too often thought students who misbehaved and/or who had problems learning should be placed into special education classes as soon as possible. That is not exactly accurate. It was not that they were convinced the special education classes were the appropriate place for the students; it was more that they simply did not want the students in their class and the only option was to send the students to another class. It that other class happened to be a special education class, so be it.

On one occasion about halfway through the school year, I was shocked when I entered the assistant principal's office. When I later told my supervisor about this situation, he simply did not believe me until I produced the evidence. Unbelievably the assistant principal had all third-grade teachers fill out testing referral forms for every student in their classes! That's right; the assistant principal referred the entire third grade for testing! By way of explanation, she said she was receiving multiple complaints from all of the third teachers about the behavior of the students. I had firsthand knowledge of the third-grade teachers and their classrooms. The classroom climates were terrible – constantly negative with the teachers yelling at the students most of the time and a general atmosphere of gloom. The teachers had no control of the classrooms and had no interest in implementing any classroom behavior strategies I suggested to them.

To the teachers in the school who cared and who worked hard, this group of third-grade teachers was an embarrassment. I wrote a memorandum to the principal about the third-grade teachers and left it in his In Box at the school. I received no response, so a couple of weeks later I slipped a copy of the memorandum under his door and knocked. No response. So finally, I put the memorandum in an envelope and convinced the secretary that the envelope contained information that the principal had requested and put on the top of his lunch tray. I stood near his office and I witnessed him take the lunch tray with the envelope perched atop. No response–ever. When I reported this absurd and troubling school to my supervisor, who was a diligent and kind professional, he said his hands were tied, which I took to mean that the central office did not care and would not make a change of leadership at the school. By the way, I did not test the entire third grade.

Two years later, the troubles of this elementary school could not be ignored any longer. Parents and child advocates finally gathered enough strength and influence to force the central office to pay attention to the school. The indifferent principal retired, and a new principal was selected. She was a highly intelligent, very attractive lady with a dynamic personality who loved children and was determined to provide them with a quality school experience. She told me later that when she was selected as the school's principal, her supervisor told her "*Do what you can.*" Clearly, the expectations remained low.

The transformation of that school was remarkable to witness after she arrived. She started with the climate of the school. She believed that a positive school climate is foundational – that's where school improvement begins.

She cleaned up the building, cleaned out the teachers who were incompetent or who did not have the best interests of the students in mind, cleared out the assistant principal (and sanitized the office), fired the custodians, and opened the school doors to parents and the business community. She went into the homes of the students, developed after-school activities, created tutoring sessions for failing students, and created professional learning opportunities for the staff that focused on instruction, classroom behavior, school climate, classroom climate, and motivation. Her school received several mini-grants from businesses and non-profit agencies that provided fresh paint, pictures, plants, and motivational plaques throughout the school. Volunteers routinely cleaned up the campus and the building. Teachers felt supported, encouraged, and the level of professional expectations elevated so teachers felt proud of and were recognized for their work. School climate improved dramatically, which led to improved student behavior and increased student achievement.

The new principal was seldom in her office. She was in the hallways, in the classrooms, in the cafeteria, and she was always speaking to and encouraging students and teachers. She brought community leaders and business leaders into the school to speak to and work with students. The principal was recognized and praised for her work by teachers, parents, and others. However, she kept the heat on the central office about school supplies, textbooks, furniture, quality teachers, quality staff, and anything and everything she needed to make the school the best it could be for all students.

I saw her and other teachers greet students in the morning and say goodbye each afternoon. They knew the students so well they could tell when a student was in a bad mood, was sad, or disturbed about something. They would pull students aside and offer encouragement or walk them to the counseling suite.

I was there one morning when a student was brought to the principal by a teacher. The student was crying her heart out. She said her mother was sick and they had no way to go to the doctor. The principal called me over and asked me to ride with her to the student's house. The school nurse went with us. When we arrived at the house, we found a tiny house with broken window screens, a dirt yard, and a narrow swirl of smoke drifting from a small fireplace. When we went in, we were greeted by an emaciated woman who was clearly very ill. It was difficult to guess her age because of her physical condition. When the principal told her that we were going to call an ambulance, she protested bitterly. She croaked that she had no insurance and no money and no clothes to wear to the hospital. We all reassured her that was not a problem. The principal rode in the ambulance with the mother and her young daughter rode with us to the hospital. All along the way, the little girl cried that her mother was going to be upset with her.

The emergency room took the mother in immediately. We waited with her daughter. About two hours later a doctor visited with us. She asked the little girl if she had relatives nearby. She said no. The doctor asked to speak with us, so the school nurse stayed with the girl. With a heavy heart, the doctor said the mother who was only 39 years old had tuberculosis and cancer. She gave her only a few weeks to live and added that she would never leave the hospital. Of course, the little girl was devastated and hysterical when the principal told her. She was heartbroken about losing her mother and terrified because she didn't know what would happen to her without her mother. We contacted the Department of Family and Children Services to secure the little girl's future because obviously, she could not go back to the house, except to retrieve the few meager things she had there. The principal received permission from the mother and DFCS to take the little girl into her home temporarily. She lived with the principal for several months while DFCS looked for a foster family that lived close to the school. The school essentially adopted the little girl and filled her life with love and support.

The principal was a servant leader who made others around her feel connected and important. The servant leader was first described and identified by Robert Greenleaf who said,

It begins with the natural feeling that one wants to serve, to serve first. Then conscious choice brings one to aspire to lead. The difference manifests itself in the care taken by the servant-first to make sure that other people's highest priority needs are being served.

Servant leadership includes various methods of frequent communications and focuses on the health of the workplace by constantly taking stock of the cleanliness and safety of the facility and by interacting frequently with staff members.

It is clear from research that when leadership is dysfunctional and dictatorial, motivation and productivity levels plummet and effective communications are absent. The principal knew that communications were critically important to the climate of the school.

Two years after turning the school around, the principal was visited by a deputy superintendent who told her another school needed her. The principal told me later that her heart was broken because she loved the school and the community. She said; however, she would gather herself together and transform the other school, too. The students, faculty, and community were shocked and saddened when they learned their beloved principal was leaving.

When she arrived unannounced at her new assignment she was shocked at the condition of the school. The school was a mess just like the one she turnaround. She saw trash in the parking lot; broken parking signs; cracked school windows; dirty hallway floors; stinking bathrooms; and many other indications of a neglected school. When she walked into the front office, none of the secretaries greeted her or even acknowledged her presence. She stood patiently at the front counter for several minutes with a cordial smile on her face. A secretary finally looked up at her but then went back to her magazine. The principal said out loud in a strong, clear voice: *"I'm the new principal of this school and I want every one of you to pack your personal belongings and report to the school system's Human Resources (HR) Department immediately. You are no longer employed in this school*." All of them looked at her and then each other and then back at her in stunned silence. One said, "*You can't do that*." The principal said, "*If you're not out of here in 10 minutes or less, I will call the police to escort you out*." That motivated them to leave.

She spent the day going to each classroom and what she saw was worse than anything she'd ever seen in a school. She visited the cafeteria staff and the kitchen area. She told the staff they had 10 minutes to clean everything spotless or she would terminate all of them. She could not find the custodian. She looked everywhere and asked several people about his whereabouts. Some teachers said he never works, and he is never available to help them. She went to the employee parking lot and found the custodian asleep in his car. She called the HR Department and asked that someone visit the school immediately. When the custodial staff supervisor from HR followed her to the car, he jerked the car door open and announced, "*You're fired*." It took the principal months to clean up the school and she had more resistance from the teachers than in the previous school. However, she garnered the support of parents and a core of teachers who were sick of the negative school climate and demanded changes. When the principal faced resistance from HR getting rid of some incompetent teachers, she turned to the parents and the other teachers, who then flooded their local board representatives with phone calls.

The principal asked me to work with teachers on classroom climate and student behavior even though that was not one of my assigned schools. I coordinated with another school psychologist that was assigned to the school and we had very productive sessions with small groups of teachers and with individual teachers. We paired excellent teachers with struggling teachers. That was the best device to improve classroom and ultimately school climate. The principal gave teachers strong leadership roles and opportunities to identify and correct problems in the school. She asked the teachers to decide what type of professional learning they wanted and needed and she arranged for the sessions.

Several teachers at her former school asked to transfer to her new school because teachers want strong leaders who support them and who care about children.

CHAPTER 22
PRINCIPALS–PITIFUL OR POWERFUL

I didn't really dislike school. It was the principal of the thing.

-Henny Youngman

The superintendent of one of the largest school districts in the country personally visits every community where a principal vacancy is being filled to ask the community, parents, and staff what they want in their new principal. The superintendent takes the HR director and staff with him and they take notes of the comments in the public meeting. The superintendent oversees the principal selection process himself. That's probably why the school district continues to outperform other similar school districts and has for years. One of his top priorities is ensuring that the principal candidate can articulate the importance of school climate. He also has a keen "bully detector" about a potential principal. He always says that a bully principal creates conditions in a school that jeopardize teaching and learning.

In their groundbreaking book *"Breaking the Silence,"* Jo and Joseph Blasé addressed the problem of the abusive, bullying principal. They interviewed elementary, middle/junior high, and high school teachers from rural, suburban, and urban areas across the United States and Canada and wrote the following,

It is clear that working in an abusive environment causes considerable harm to teachers, classrooms, and schools

as a whole. For mistreated teachers, as for employees in other fields of work, such environments create fear and mistrust, resentment, hostility, feelings of humiliation, withdrawal, play-it-safe strategies, and hiding mistakes. The bottom-line consequences of mistreatment of teachers by principals are clear ... teachers who fell victim to abusive principals responded with depressed commitment and loyalty to their schools, they did the minimum amount of work to get by, and they feared and avoided all interactions with their principals.

I had the unpleasant experience of working with a bully principal during my first year on the job. When I arrived one fall morning at an elementary school shaded by beautiful ancient oak trees and surrounded by a low-income neighborhood, I reported to the main office. I was greeted by a scarecrow of a secretary whose shifting eyes reminded me of a trapped animal. The principal's office door was closed but I could hear loud voices coming from the office. I could not understand what was being said but it was clear by the reaction of the secretary that she was fearful of something. Her eyes kept shifting from the principal's office to me and back and forth. She said since I did not have an appointment, she was not sure if the principal would see me. I told her I would only take a minute. I just wanted to introduce myself to the principal and let him know I would be the school psychologist assigned to his school for the school year. I thought meeting the principal before walking around the school was the courteous way to handle introductions. A short time later, a person emerged from the principal's office wiping tears from her eyes, visibly upset. Keep in mind, this was a pre-planning week – the week before school starts that teachers use to prepare their classrooms and lesson plans. In fact, this was the first day of pre-planning and yet a teacher was already being reprimanded about something.

After I watched her leave the office, I turned back around to see the principal glaring at me from his doorway. A short, somewhat stocky pock-faced man with a raspy voice with a snarl on his lips said, *"And what do you want?"* I could tell this school had a negative school climate. Before I could answer, he shot an accusing look at the waif-like secretary who quickly looked down and trembled. When I stood, he turned and went back into his office. I followed him, which greatly alarmed and panicked the secretary who was shaking her head as I walked toward the principal's office as if warning me not to go in uninvited.

Being young, stupid, and with a little bit of an edge has its unintended advantages sometimes. This was one of those times because the principal was clearly startled when he saw that I had followed him into his office. *"Who are you?"* he blurted out in somewhat of a stammer. I had plenty of experience with bullies of all shapes and sizes and ages throughout my entire life. My childhood neighborhood was not exactly a replica of the "Leave It to Beaver" neighborhood. We did not have gangs, we had thugs and bullies. So, I recognize a bully very quickly and I had learned a long time ago that the best way to deal with a bully is to go straight at them. This guy was clearly a bully and a coward.

When I introduced myself, he said: *"I don't like you and your manner, and I don't think it's important whether or not you like me."* I had worked hard to get to that point in my life, and my life up to that point had not always been easy. I had dealt with tough, mean-spirited, and even cruel individuals. I knew what it was like to be alienated, cast off, and dispirited. So even though I was brand new to the job and thankful that I had a job and I was trying to make a good impression to keep my job, this guy pissed me off.

I was in many ways still naïve, but I knew a snake when I saw one and this guy qualified. I stood up, took a step closer to his desk and told him that it does indeed matter whether or not we like each other because we had to work together. He did not say a word. I stared at him for a moment and then I said, "*Have a good day.*" I left his office, but before I left, I turned to him and said: "*And don't take it out on your secretary.*" I added, "*She was very professional and told me not to enter your office unless I was invited. I chose to do otherwise, so don't blame her.*"

As I drove off toward another school, I had two thoughts: (1) the principal is probably on the phone to my supervisor to file a complaint against me and (2) why did I accept a job in this school district.

As I worked in his school that year, our interactions were strictly professional and straight forward. The teachers feared him and avoided him, just like Blasé findings. These teachers were also more prone to bully their students. We received many complaints in that school about teachers intimidating students. It was learned behavior from the principal and symptomatic of the stress the teachers were under. I tried working with the teachers, but most were fearful, burned or stressed out, and all had a negative attitude toward the principal. Teacher attendance was negatively impacted, which jeopardized the continuity of instruction. Needless to say, that school was a depressing place for students and teachers. The school climate was completely negative.

In some cases, the injury caused by principals led to the virtual undoing of dedicated and caring professional educators, all of whom viewed teaching as a special calling. (Blasé)

An article titled "*A Toxic Leader Manifesto*" by Alan Goldman describes the role and outcome of destructive leadership and how that type of leadership style creates a negative workplace climate. Goldman challenges toxic leaders in a sarcastic tone. If a leader is determined to be destructive; if that seems to be the only way to lead an organization, Goldman wants, with tongue-in-cheek, to make sure that type of leader does it "correctly." Although Goldman is approaching the topic in a sarcastic manner, there are many essential and meaningful points to gain from his "manifesto" because it adroitly characterizes all that is wrong with a toxic leader.

It is essential to bypass dialogue and question and answers; the leader must attack, deflate or discard employees who are identified as lacking in any way or who dare challenge the leader; bullying must be cultivated and perfected; the leader must yell at and demean employees who fall short, error or are deemed annoying; the leader must stifle any workplace conversation that questions the leader; all attacks against employees must be brought forth into public forums for all to witness; it is mandatory to yell at employees in an effort to promote fear, humiliation and sufficient loss of face; when criticizing employees the leader must carry this forth harshly and publicly without any opportunity for the offending employee to respond, and the destructive leader must remember that civilized and substantive feedback is his mortal enemy.

Research on destructive leadership can be found in Lipman-Blumen's book, *The Allure of Toxic Leaders*, which addresses why employees follow the toxic or destructive leader-typically from a basic need to survive, which supports the findings of Blasé. Employee compliance gives the leader the false impression that he is a good leader and virtually everything he does is appropriate; therefore, the leader believes that his leadership style is effective in the organization. That is so often true with teachers in a closed environment like a school where the principal is so powerful and can be demanding. He sees employees being compliant; he sees employees implementing his policies without question, and he hears no criticism of his leadership style or any feedback from his staff that suggests the conditions in the workplace are negative. Teachers are afraid and some of them exhibit symptoms of trauma – depression, forgetfulness, neurotic tendencies, panic attacks, withdrawal, and less regard for their personal appearance and little if any focus on classroom climate

Many times, the internal negative determinants of an organization like a school are hidden by an illusion of productivity. In this scenario, the central office assumes that the principal is really "shaking things up" and, consequently, improvement and success cannot be far away.

Lipman-Blumen found that some employees think a strong, dominating, overbearing, cruel leader is attractive and necessary. Typically, employees who fall into this category are those that either fear retaliation or who believe that leadership is defined by toughness. However, there are employees with so little self-respect and self-confidence perhaps from experience or internal turmoil they think they deserve someone that is cruel and insensitive. And, of course, there are employees who think being an insensitive and bullying leader fits their preferred style of management, so they view the totalitarian leader as a role model.

After working there for several months, some of the teachers trusted me enough to talk about the awful working climate at the school. They wanted me to do something. I tried to explain my limits, but one day I witnessed an event that sent me over the edge.

I walked into the teachers' lounge one afternoon and found a teacher doubled over crying. I ran to her to see if she was okay, was she hurt, was she sick, did she need a doctor? She shook her head without looking up and continued to cry. I sat next to her. Another teacher came in and looked at me. I just shook my head and lifted my shoulders to indicate I didn't know what was wrong. The teacher knelt in from of the crying teacher and softly called her name as she took her hands into hers. The teacher looked up slowly with tears streaming down her face and the most haunting look in her eyes and said she can't work there any longer, but she has to have a job. About that time the principal walked into the lounge and barked out loud, "*What's going on here?*" The crying teacher froze, and panic was on her face. The other teacher stood up and said,

"*Ms. D. doesn't feel well and we're making sure she's okay.*" The principal practically shouted, "*We don't have time for teachers to get sick around here. You'll need to get back to work right now.*" The other teacher said, "*We're leaving in a minute.*" That infuriated the principal who said, "*Leave now or get out of the school.*" I stayed out of it up until that point, but his callousness stung me. I stood up and said to the principal, "*I need to talk to you*" as I blocked his view of the teachers. It was obviously to divert his attention away from the two teachers. The veteran teacher immediately understood and swept the other teacher out the side door. In the hallway, I said to the principal, "*How much longer do you think creating a hostile workplace is going to go unnoticed?*" He became furious and sputtered, "*Are you threatening me?*" I said, "*If you want to take it that way, yes.*" He stormed off but not before he threatened to get me fired.

That afternoon I reported what happened to my supervisor. I didn't expect him to do much except warn me to tread softly when working in that school. Instead, he took me to the Dragon Lady who ran the division like a Marine Drill Sergeant and was not sympathetic to anyone or any circumstances. I thought she would turn on me and make this my problem. Going to her office was the last place I wanted to go, but my supervisor asked me to retell the story to her. She crossed her arms and said, "*The principal really handled that situation like that?*" I said not only that situation; he intimidated all staff members, students, and parents. I told her the students and teachers in the school did not have a chance and we should all be troubled about how that experience can negatively impact the lives of those students and teachers for years thereafter. To my surprise, the Dragon Lady said, *"I'm going to pay our friend a visit."* It's interesting that one bully quickly observed and denounced another bully, which she did. She offered a scathing report of the conditions of the school to the HR department and the principal was eventually moved to a non-leadership position.

But the principal had been there for years. I wonder how many of those teachers remained in the profession after spending time with that worthless principal. I have also thought about how students who grew to dislike school there would have done had they attended a school with a nurturing and caring principal and a positive school climate.

The other principals I worked with that year ranged from mediocre to effective, from innovative to insignificant, from stable to unstable. Some were a combination and contradiction of all of the above.

Another principal comes to mind. He was effective but very mercurial. He was bright but peculiar. One of many examples was his "light bulb" routine. He would not let me use any part of the building for testing students except a small book room that no longer contained textbooks because it was too damp. He thought it was the quietest place in the building for testing. If that was not strange enough, the worst part was that he made me check out and check in a light bulb when I came to the school to test students. So, understand this routine. I would go to the front office of the school upon arriving in the morning to sign in. The secretary, a delightful ancient, would greet me and open a file cabinet that housed my 60 watts light bulb. I received my light bulb with a smile and "thank you" and then I proceeded to the damp book room. I stood in a chair and screwed in the light bulb and looked for a paper wad to put under the wobbly table. I left the door open to let fresh air in and to relieve the room of the musty odor. The rest of the day was spent working with students in the room. The highlight of the day was when I went to classrooms to observe students. At the end of the day, I turned the light off and give the light bulb time to cool off and then in reverse order the light bulb would end up safely secured in the secretary's file cabinet. The principal saw nothing peculiar about this arrangement.

Before shaking your head at the principal's bizarre attitude about the light bulb consider this story. He surprised me one day when he asked me to speak at the school's next PTA meeting. The topic was "How Schools Can Help Families." I was told I had 15 minutes. I worked hard with the advice from my colleagues to create a visual presentation that I hoped would be useful to parents.

Considering that it was a bitterly cold night, the number of parents who attended that PTA meeting was very impressive. The meeting was held in the school cafeteria, a common setting for PTA meetings. They heard children sing and the school staff provided refreshments. The parents heard from the school counselor, some teachers, and the principal gave a very impressive speech about the school and the importance of parents to the success of a school. Prior to his arrival at the school as principal, parent participation was declining. He made a concentrated effort to reach out to parents and it seemed to be working. After the principal spoke, he turned it over to me. I had the attention of the parents as I talked about the developmental stages of children and different learning styles. Then we moved to the question and answer time of my presentation. There were a few questions about parenting, about the testing process, about developmental stages of children, and such. During this Q and A time, I kept noticing a little rustling and heads turning toward the back of the audience, as if some parents were being distracted or were upset by someone in the audience. It was not a loud or noticeable disturbance, just a quiet murmur. Suddenly, a lady in the back of the room stood up and said, *"We have all Black children in this school, and I want to know what you think you know about Black children since you've been White all of your life?"* Before I could even let the question sink in, the other parents started shouting her down and then the principal jumped up and said, *"Mr. McGiboney has worked with our children all year and he treats them all with respect. I've had parents comment on his kindness and willingness to talk to them. Mam, if you have an issue, you take it up with me."* The parents broke out in applause for their principal. He then came over to me in front of everyone and shook my hand. He wanted the parents to see, as well as the students who were in the auditorium, a Black man and a White man work together.

Several parents came up to me after the meeting to shake my hand and compliment my presentation. It was my first public presentation in my professional life, and it mattered, and the parents and the principal made it memorable. The next time I visited that school the principal said I could use the study room in the media center instead of the damp bookroom. He shook my hand and said simply, *"You handled that situation very well."* He was the one that handled the situation very well.

In a Wallace Foundation six-year study reported in *Education Week*, surveys of over 8,400 teachers, 470 building administrators and 1,000 district and state level leaders, 300 plus classroom observations and an analysis of student test scores in mathematics and English revealed that principal leadership has a significant influence on student learning.

Some of the findings and recommendations include:

- *Successful principals set conditions and the school's climate that enable teachers to be better instructors. Principals in low achieving schools exhibited the lowest amount of instructional leadership behavior.*
- *Elementary school principals exhibited more instructional leadership behaviors than secondary school principals. While secondary school principals delegated these behaviors to department chairpersons, there was no evidence that these teachers provided instructional leadership as effectively as the principals, because the principal created the conditions for learning – the school climate.*
- *Principals need time to develop effective partnerships among leadership staff, teachers and parents; therefore, principal transfers need to be carefully thought through.*
- *Districts should think carefully before moving a 'star' principal to a low performing school because the 'last' school may then have problems and there are no guarantees that success in one school automatically transfers to another school.*

- *Professional development for principals needs to be a needs-driven, on-going, and iterative effort conducted locally that focuses on school climate and workplace conditions.*
- *The most effective principals are able to use data and show teachers how to use data in the decision-making process and through instruction. They establish the purposes and expectations for data use and then provide both collegial training sessions in the use of data and follow-up assistance and encourage peer-to-peer exchanges of ideas.*
- *The most effective principals understand the importance of school climate and how important it is to nurture a positive school climate.*

The extreme range of principal quality was prevalent throughout my many years in public education. The good news is that a good principal creates a school climate that is positive and productive. Consequently, students learn and develop and teachers and other staff members can focus on their jobs because they feel important and needed, and parents are involved in the school. The bad news is that a bad principal can damage a school climate, intimidate teachers, alienate parents, and ignore or negatively impact students. All of which ultimately affects all of the necessary components that lead to student development, student achievement, and effective teaching.

A UCLA study used a school climate survey to investigate the relationship between a school's climate and student achievement. The survey had six factors: collaborative leadership; teacher collaboration; professional development; unity of purpose; collegial support; and learning partnership. The study shows how student performance in both math and language arts is positively correlated with a collaborative, caring school climate. They also found that the climate of a school depends in large part on the leadership of the principal.

Stanford University researchers and The Wallace Foundation released a report, *Preparing School Leaders for a Changing World*. The report *"recognizes the close link between the quality of school leadership and school performance."*

The findings show that high-performing principals are not just born but can be made and that those who are prepared in innovative, high-quality programs are more likely to become instructional leaders who are committed to the job and efficacious in their work.

The UCLA and Stanford University studies do not vary greatly from the studies of school leadership by the Education Research Information Center (ERIC). According to ERIC, there have been over 10,000 publications over the past 30 years on school leadership. The common thread through all of the research is the effectiveness or ineffectiveness of the principal and how it relates to the mission of public education and measurable outcomes for students that are related to the school climate that the principal establishes and endorses through his actions.

After all of these years and after all of the research, the fact remains that the quality of education in any public school is based on the effectiveness of the principal and teachers. The principal selects the teachers, supervises the teachers, establishes the climate of the school, the quality of the day-to-day operations, and so much more. But this is not where it ends. As Norman Vincent Peale once wrote, *"Any fact facing us is not as important as our attitude toward it, for that determines our success or failure."*

The fact is we know a good principal can make a public school good and a bad principal can make a public school bad. The problem is complacency toward that fact. Why does public education not focus more of its efforts on ensuring that competent principals are in every public school? Why does higher education not play a more significant role in training principals? It is a perfect example of a system that weakens itself through internal politics, nepotism, naïve notions of leadership, favoritism, faulty interview and selection processes, and stubbornness.

The American Supervision and Curriculum Development published *Qualities of Effective Principals* that serves as both guidelines for those selecting and training principals as well as guidelines for practicing principals on effective practices. Yet, throughout the United States, local superintendents, and local boards of education will pay little attention to guidelines of this nature when selecting a principal or when evaluating a principal.

I have worked with hundreds of principals throughout my career. I have seen the best and the worst. I have mentioned a few of the principals I worked with, but another story illustrates what good leadership can mean to a school and its community.

In the poorest part of the school district, in an elementary school tucked away in a residential area filled with tiny houses built in the 1940s and '50s and narrow streets, I met a principal who over the years was the standard to which I compared other principals.

When I drove to the school for the first time, I developed a mental picture of the school as I drove through the neighborhood of old homes in various conditions of repair. Some were taken care of while others were noticeably neglected. I pictured a rundown, old school building, but that is not what I found. As I turned the last corner near the school, I saw before me an old elementary school building built in 1949 resting on a gentle rise with majestic oaks trees hovering over the school like protective parents. The school lawn was carefully cut and trimmed at the edges along the walkways. The bushes bordering the perimeter of the school building were trimmed to perfection. The trim of the building was freshly painted. Pots of flowers greeted students, staff, and parents at the stairs leading to the main entrance. A new marquee shared a "Thought of the Week" and school information. A welcome center manned by a parent greeted me in the lobby filled with artwork, books of poetry, posters of famous people in history and literature, and soft classical music filled the air throughout the school. Inside, the building was spotless. The floors had that high gloss shine that radiates light and denotes a sense of pride. The restrooms were clean and were obviously cleaned several times during the school day. Each restroom had fresh flowers. The front office was filled with plants and flowers and information booklets for parents on topics such as nutrition, parenting, community services, homework, etc. The school secretary greeted me with a sincere smile and professional greeting and welcome, as she did with everyone who entered the school. I saw teachers smiling and interacting positively with each other and students and parents, and none of this was an illusion; it happened every day.

Every morning the principal and the assistant principal met each student and staff member at the front door with a warm and cheerful greeting. The administrative staff was often in the classrooms, not just to observe teachers but to offer assistance to the teachers. Some of the teachers had less than three years of experience; consequently, the principal and the assistant principal were conducting staff development almost daily in the classrooms to help and encourage the teachers.

The principal had a clear mission in mind for me. He made it clear that he needed me to assist teachers and work with parents, not just test students. That may not sound exactly revolutionary now, but in those days school psychologists were viewed primarily as "testers." In fact, the principal's expectation conflicted with my supervisor's expectations. All of the school psychologists in the school district had a weekly "testing quota." No matter the circumstances, we had to test at least 12 students per week. It did not matter what other services a school might need. It did not matter what other services students and parents and teachers might need. It did not matter if a school psychologist had a resistant or difficult student to work with. It did not matter if one or two of the assigned schools had emergencies during the week. What mattered only were the 12 evaluations each week.

When I explained the testing quota to the school principal, I had no way to predict or anticipate his reaction. He was a soft-spoken, kind-hearted, thoughtful person, but he was passionate about what was best for students and staff. His response was totally unexpected. He said that he understood the quotas and he understood my dilemma. He went on to say that he has teachers who need assistance and he has students and parents who need help. *"If you can live with yourself knowing that you can help others and you choose not to,"* he said, *"then meet your testing quotas."*

I felt like I had been hit in my chest, but his aim was at my heart. He made the choice clear – no drama, no preaching, no tirade, no concessions. Be an effective, caring professional or be a tester, a person with a kit, test forms, and quotas. It was my decision.

I worked with teachers on classroom management; I conducted small group sessions with acting-out students; I started a parent's group, and I even met my testing quota some of the time. What a wonderful school to work in. What a wonderfully positive school climate. I wanted to work there every day. Students were learning and enjoying school in a clean, safe building with an energetic staff and a positive, caring principal. When stuff happened, like a fire in the ceiling one morning, the students and staff handled it in stride. When a parent came into the school very angry, the principal and other staff members knew how to calm him or her down. After the heartbreak of a student's death in a car accident, the school pulled together like a family, visiting the family, offering donations of time, money, and other comforts. If children came to school without a coat during winter, the principal found volunteers to collect and give away coats. It was not a school without problems, and it was not a school without issues and challenges, but it was a successful public school in a poor neighborhood. And the catalyst for the school's success was the principal and the positive school climate he created.

When I turned toward his expectation of me and the services I would provide at this school, he was very supportive. He made certain that I had a comfortable room in which to work with students, parents, and teachers. If there were any types of problems, he was there to listen and offer advice. Sometimes, he asked me to work with a student based on his own observations or after he talked with parents.

One time he asked me to work with a student new to the school. The little first-grade boy was a very angry child who pushed and hit other students and did not listen to his teacher. In his first week at school, he was brought to the principal's office several times, so the principal had a parent conference. The parents did not know what to do with their little boy either. They were poor and often moved from one place to another. However, the father said he found a job close by that seemed to offer some stability for him and his family, so he expected to remain in the neighborhood for a long time. They were renting a small house near the school.

I worked with the little boy and as a team, the school implemented some behavior management strategies that seem to work reasonably well with the student. The teachers noticed that the morning hours were the worst time of the day for the boy – when he was irritable and aggressive. So, when I had a follow-up parent conference, we talked a lot about parenting-related issues. The mother said it would be helpful if they could meet with me on a regular basis for a while to learn more about parenting their only child. The father agreed, but he was not exactly enthusiastic about the idea. So, we met once a week at a time that did not interfere with his job or her job. She worked a part-time job from 8:00 am to 11:00 am. He worked a night shift, going in at 3:00 pm and of course he would sleep late in the morning, so we met at 1:00 pm on Fridays. It did not take long, nor did it take any special training to determine why the morning was the toughest part of the little boy's day. His father was trying to sleep when the little boy and his mother were rushing about the house trying to get ready for school and work. Inevitably they would make too much noise and wake the father, who would start yelling at them and then he could not go back to sleep. That was what the little boy faced each morning of the school week. No wonder he was ready to hit somebody by the time he got to school.

We talked about that during the sessions and we also talked about many other issues that troubled this couple. They both had a very tough life with many more downs than ups. Their marriage hung together by a thread at times and the sessions sometimes became very emotional for them as the main topic of parenting shifted to marital and financial issues. I listened mostly and sometimes guided the conversation away from confrontation and toward communications. Sometimes I had to confront the father's bullying tactics toward his wife. For several months, we met every week. In the meantime, their little boy adjusted to school because his teachers were wonderful and because the principal became the little boy's mentor.

As we were closing up our last session of the school year, the father said to me as he stood up to leave, *"You were pretty rough with me sometimes."* I just smiled. *"But my boy is doing better, and my wife doesn't fuss as much, which is a good thing. I don't guess you know I carry a gun with me at all times. In those meetings with you, I felt like pulling it out on you a couple of times."* He smiled and pulled up one pants leg to show me a .25 caliber handgun strapped to his calf. I did not smile. I am not sure I breathed. He chuckled as he walked down the hallway hand-in-hand with his wife.

Later that day I told the principal. He told me to sit down and we talked for a long time. He knew I was completely shocked by what had happened and what could have happened had the father gone for his gun inside the school. It was a frightening thought, but the principal reassured me that the father would never do that; he was just playing with me. The principal was like that all of the time, which seems impossible, but I never saw him shout at anybody, lose his temper, overreact in any way or act downtrodden about anything, and he always had time to talk to his staff. His teachers adored and admired him. He wanted and expected his school to be a good place for students, parents, teachers, other staff members, and visitors.

Destructive leadership takes a significant toll on morale and productivity. Studies show that over 40 percent of American employees, regardless of the type of work they do, classify their jobs as stressful and 75 percent of employees said the most stressful part of their job is the behavior and attitude of their immediate supervisor. Studies also indicate that many employees would prefer a more conducive, healthy, and positive workplace over a higher salary. These same studies point to workplace climate as a reflection of leadership.

In the book *The Classic Touch*, the authors speak about a basic failing of many leaders–the failure to encourage their managers to show good manners and courtesy to all employees while creating and nurturing a positive workplace climate.

From the history of leadership, according to the authors, going back centuries, even during violent times the most effective leaders showed respect for others. Caesar understood the importance of connecting with and trusting his staff as well as the soldiers. He could and would be demanding and did not shy away from correcting his immediate officers, but then he would later talk with them one-on-one or in front of others to point out how important the person's work was to the Roman Empire.

As I mentioned before, some principals and central office leaders are disciples of *Machiavellian* leadership style, based on the mistaken belief that it is better to be feared than loved because there is more security in fear than in love. Machiavellian leadership in precise terms is the effort to utilize manipulative tactics and endorse a cynical, untrustworthy view of human nature.

In a recent study of the impact of Machiavellian leadership on employees, the researchers found that the overbearing nature of the leadership style resulted in higher levels of emotional exhaustion among employees.

I saw that in schools led by principals who were overbearing, uncaring, manipulative, intimidating, and who had created a negative school climate.

The good news about leadership is that effective leaders share common traits that can be taught and reinforced:

1. *Set a good example for others – A leader's attitude is contagious. Communication is key to making members of the organization feel included in major decisions. Employees are more motivated when they feel needed, appreciated, and valued.*

2. *Focus on employee happiness and work satisfaction rather than employee motivation. Successful leaders focus on the "happiness factor" for employees and customers. For example, workplace climates that include humor are strong on camaraderie and production.*

3. *It's important to make sure employees share in the organization's successful projects – An employee's performance, productivity, and motivation can be linked to how invested he feels in the work, which depends considerably on feedback and acknowledgment that his work is noticed and is meaningful.*

4. *Leaders should encourage employees to share what is working and what is not working. This is an effective means of heading off problems and working toward continuous improvement, but the effectiveness is based on a positive workplace climate.*

Very few leaders are born with all of the skills and attitude necessary to be a successful leader. There are some "natural leaders" but most effective leaders are created in the cauldron of life's experiences and what they learned and how they merge those experiences with their respect for people.

CHAPTER 23
SEND IN THE CLOWN

You do not lead by hitting people over the head – that's assault, not leadership.

-Dwight Eisenhower

I should make one technical correction at this point. It was not my immediate supervisor who dogmatically set the psychological testing quotas; it was his supervisor. She was a stern, unapproachable person who believed in management by fear. I earlier referred to her as the Dragon Lady.

She had mastered the principles of management by fear and intimidation. She also understood the power of humiliation, especially the demonstrated power of humiliation coupled with overt shows of fearlessness. Her staff meetings were very intimidating by design. Everyone had to sit in the front and only God could help you if you were late to a staff meeting. That indiscretion was always followed by a screaming individual conference after public humiliation. She deliberately gave the impression that no one could do anything right.

One winter night we had several inches of sleet and freezing rain, which is very unusual for the Deep South. At that time, I lived several miles from the central office. We had a staff meeting scheduled with the Dragon Lady at 7:30 a.m. the next morning. I had to leave my house no later than 6:00 a.m. to make it in time for her meeting. Driving on ice is a challenge, so I left even earlier. About 30 minutes later I heard on the car radio that my school district was closed due to icy road conditions. I was already over half way to work so I continued to work and let myself in the building. I worked most of the day and left in the early afternoon. Our staff meeting was rescheduled for the next day.

The next day, Dragon Lady started the meeting off with this: *"We have a staff member who came to work yesterday despite the school district being closed and despite the icy road conditions."* She went on with that line of comment for several minutes with an even tone. I was blushing with pride, particularly because I had never heard her praise anybody. After she finished her description of my efforts, she said, *"And I want all of you to know that the person who drove to work on dangerous roads was none other than our own Garry McGiboney."* I was proud. She was going to compliment me in public. Then she said, *"Mr. McGiboney, that was the dumbest damn thing I have ever heard of and you should be ashamed for using such poor judgment. How stupid can you be? Nobody is impressed with what you did, and if you think doing that was going to impress me, you're dumber than I thought."*

Of course, I was humiliated, angry, and demoralized. For those in education who have not figured this out yet, even after all of the examples I've offered in this book, here is some solid advice: that type of leadership style does not work. It never has worked, and it never will work. I do not recall seeing any courses or books on leadership that advocates leadership-by-humiliation, but I have seen too many examples of that type of leadership in public education and in other places.

I have been accused of being passively aggressive at times. Admittedly, there are examples of my behavior that tend to support that accusation. The Dragon Lady was prim and proper and basically the classic prude. So, in my own passive-aggressive manner, I sent her an Eastern Onion Sing-a-Gram for her birthday with instructions to send a person dressed in a clown costume to sing Happy Birthday to her. I knew that would affront every fiber of her being. Word got around the office what was going to happen. On that day when the singing telegram clown walked into the building, the building and parking lot emptied of employees. Fear and panic gripped the masses and they left. I stayed. I watched the singer come into the building through the back door, per my instructions, where I was there to make sure he knew which office to go into. I went back to my cubicle after watching the clown angle into the Dragon Lady's office. A few seconds passed and then very faintly I could hear a soft but clear singing voice. In a matter of seconds, that true, delicate voice was drowned out by a shriek not of this world. You could literally hear the scream of outrage throughout the entire building. The first thing that came to my mind was the sound of a banshee, the female spirit in Gaelic folklore believed to presage, by wailing, a death in a family. The death, in this case, was going to most likely be my own. The singer ran from the building, with pieces of his costume falling away as he crashed through the exit door.

I could feel the temperature in the building rise as the Dragon Lady stalked the halls looking for a victim. I did not move. My phone rang, but I did not answer it. The building was so quiet I could hear my heart stop. The velociraptor was on the prowl. The sound of her high heels clicked at a rapid pace as she went up and then down the halls looking for someone, anyone to attack. I am sure she was drooling through clenched teeth with seething anger.

When I heard the click of her heels slowly fade as she checked the other side of the building, I made my getaway.

The Dragon Lady's investigation led to no suspects, apparently. A short time later, a memorandum was sent to all school district employees prohibiting the use of singing telegrams. I am certain that was just a coincidence. But the story did not end there as I hoped.

One late afternoon several weeks later, when the story of the incident had made its way around the school district, a shadow stretched across my desk and I knew from the shape of the shadow that the Dragon Lady was out of her cave. I did not turn around or acknowledge her presence in any way. One does not make sudden moves when a cobra is poised to strike. I knew this was nothing but bad because she never lowered herself to visit the world of cubicles, so I knew the shadow was the shadow of death. There was no audience, so I knew instantly that she was not going to humiliate me or embarrass me. That only counts when others can see it. So, it had to be something else. Termination, a stiletto in the back, a plastic bag over my head, a syringe of perfume in my veins – something horrible for certain. She put her cold, bony hand on my shoulder and I did not know whether to turn around or just blindly accept my fate. I froze. She said in a disturbingly calm voice, *"Mr. McGiboney, I know what you did."* I remained frozen in place even after she lifted her hand from my shoulder. After several minutes, I turned around and she was gone. I did not even hear the sound of her heels clicking down the hallway. She just slithered soundlessly away.

I would like to say that was a turning point in her leadership style, but it was not. She continued to intimidate and humiliate. In fact, later that year a retired police officer attended one of our staff meetings to talk about self-defense. At that time, our offices were in a high-crime area of the county, so one of the staff members requested a safety training session from local law enforcement. The former police officer was the school district's safety officer. He was a jolly fellow but very serious about his business. He made a very good presentation about personal safety.

The officer wanted to end the presentation by demonstrating some simple self-defense maneuvers. But he made one very large mistake. He asked the Dragon Lady to help him with the demonstration. We all cringed when he selected her to come to the front of the room to participate in the demonstration. Some of us were vigorously shaking our heads "no" to him. One employee put her head in her hands and started sobbing; she knew what was going to happen. His first demonstration was to illustrate how to break away when someone grabs a person from behind, so he walked up behind the Dragon Lady and careful not to touch her he reached around her and gently grasped her arms while he was explaining every slow-motion movement. He asked the Dragon Lady what she would do in such a situation. Without hesitation and in a lightning-quick motion she crushed his right foot with her pointed shoe heel, which broke his grasp, spun around and kicked him hard in the groin. He fell to the floor in pure agony, moaning and groaning. She turned to the staff and said, *"That is all you need to know about that – dismissed and get back to work."* Then she left the room without any hint of regret, with the poor man on the floor struggling with the pain between his legs.

CHAPTER 24
MATCHES AND BENEATH THE WHEEL

Most people live lives of quiet desperation.

-Henry David Thoreau

The demands of testing quotas ended abruptly for me one rainy morning. I was summoned to the front office of the school I was working in. Thinking first that it was a family emergency imagine my shock when I heard the Dragon Lady's clipped voice instructing me to rush over to a nearby high school to see a student in "distress." When I asked about the nature of the distress, she said, *"It sounds pretty bad"* and then she hung up.

I did not have to drive far to the high school where "distress" was happening. I was met at the front door by one of the school counselors who briefly introduced herself and said, *"We don't know what to do."* *"We can't get in touch with his parents and the police said it's not within their jurisdiction."* I followed her into the counseling suite, and she took me to a small conference room. She leaned into the room and said to a person in the room that I could not see, *"Tom, this is Mr. McGiboney. He's here to talk to you."* I stepped inside the room. The room contained a bookshelf with a few books and an empty flower pot. The lighting was dim, and the blinds were closed, which together gave the room a claustrophobic feel. I walked into the room and at the far end of the room facing the wall was a very large young student in a chair pressed into the corner. Since he did not respond to the counselor in any way, I saw no purpose in calling his name. Since he was facing the wall, I quickly decided that he did not wish to talk, and he was probably struggling with self-control. Over the years since, I have noticed that mentally ill and traumatized children try to reduce their world to a manageable size. This was the case with Tom. His safe world was that corner of the room. So, I took a seat at the conference table and waited. I coughed softy or cleared my throat occasionally just to let him know I was still there. He cried softly but did not turn around in his chair or move his chair. He was clearly struggling with his demons.

About 45 minutes later, the counselor opened the door and asked what was going on. She was clearly puzzled to see Tom in the same position and me at the conference table. I politely and quietly asked her to leave and not to disturb us again unless Tom's parents showed up.

I had the sense we would have to start over because of the intrusion. I was right. Tom remained in that same position for another 45 minutes. During this time, I was thinking of every way possible to connect with Tom. I was pulling hard on my memory to retrieve every bit of information I gleaned in textbooks, every experience I had in training, every opportunity to learn about human behavior and mental illness I had so that I would know what to do for Tom.

The only peace I found during the time I waited on Tom was when I decided to stay with him instead of thinking about how to "cure" him or to find out what was "wrong" with him. One of our most conspicuous failings as adults is our unwillingness to listen, just listen to children. Sometimes listening and watching is more revealing than dialogue and certainly more productive than an adult monologue.

After almost two hours, Eddie turned his head ever so slightly toward me and said very softly, more like a mumble, *"You're quiet; you must be scared, too... you must know what it's like to see snakes on the wall."* Tom was fourteen years old and was on the precipice of schizophrenia.

According to the National Alliance on Mental Illness (NAMI), symptoms of schizophrenia usually begin in late adolescence or early adulthood. Numerous studies have found that about 1 in every 100 people around the world has the disorder. However, schizophrenia with an onset in adolescence (prior to age 18) is less common, and an onset of the disorder in childhood (before age 13) is exceedingly rare. It is thought that at most one in every 100 adults with schizophrenia develops it in childhood. The onset of schizophrenia in childhood sometimes is triggered by trauma or a traumatic event.

Because schizophrenia is rare at Tom's age, I was reluctant to think he had the symptoms, but after talking to his teachers, his parents, and his relatives, the signs were disturbing: hallucinations and delusions, which are firm beliefs they are out of touch with reality and which commonly include the fear that people are watching, harassing, or plotting against them; disorganized speech, which is often seen as an inability to maintain a conversation, usually as a result of difficulty staying on topic - all symptoms straight from NAMI and any authoritative text on psychiatric disorders, such as the DSM-V.

Tom was a loner because his world was not our world; his world was one of confusion, terror, and sadness. Imagine what it would be like to be afraid almost every minute of every day and to fear sleep because of nightmares. Tom expressed all of that to me and looked at me as if pleading for help. When I simply said, *"Tom, I understand that you're tired of being afraid"* he nodded affirmation and ask, *"Can you help me?"* His plea broke my heart. It took every ounce of self-control to keep from crying. When I said I would do everything possible to help, he offered a very sad smile. We sat quietly until his parents arrived, which led to tears and hugs. His parents knew something was going wrong with their son but they did not know what to do.

We were able to get Tom to a community service psychiatrist that day. Tom was later diagnosed by the psychiatrist and a psychiatric team as schizophrenic. Over time his symptoms worsened and a few years later he slipped into a catatonic state, which means he was unconscious and unresponsive and required monitoring 24/7. He remained in a psychiatric facility until his death at age 27.

Not very many days go all these many years later that I don't think about Tom and that day of quiet desperation in that conference room where he struggled so hard to capture a sane part of his otherwise insane world. There was nothing I could do. Nothing in graduate school and training covered that. There were other times working with children when there was little I could do. Accepting that was difficult.

The only thing I did in my response to the frantic directive to go to Tom's school was to show up, be patient, be there for Tom and his parents, and get him to the right professionals.

My reward for working with Tom that day was being designated as the "emergency response school psychologist" for the school district. I was pulled from testing to respond to unusual situations in the school district, and with a district that large I was called away three to four times each week. The situations ranged from sad to bizarre.

I went to a high school one afternoon because a 15-year-old girl was afraid to go home. She was afraid of what her mother might do next because she had become so unpredictable. She indicated that her mother's behavior was scaring her and she feared for her own safety and the well-being of her mother. Her mother's behavior was becoming more bizarre and unpredictable each week. She said her mother was talking to herself and then seemed confused when someone else entered the room during her self-discussions.

The scared girl said her mother threw lighted matches at her the previous night. That is when I called in a social worker to be a witness to the conversation. The girl said that she was ten minutes late coming home from her part-time job at a local fast-food restaurant and her mother accused her of being with boys. She has to walk to the restaurant and then walk home after work. On this rainy and stormy night, she was delayed by the weather. Her mother would not hear anything about an excuse for being late. As punishment, the girl was made to take her wet clothes off and stand naked in a darkened room while her mother threw lighted matches at her and chanted bible verses. She then made her daughter take a bath in a tub filled with hot water and vinegar.

The young girl was emotionally torn. She was afraid to go home, but she did not want her mother to be in trouble and she did not want to be taken away from her mother. She said it was just her and her mother. She had no other means of support and no relatives to help. She panicked when I said we would have to talk to her mother. We tried to calm her down, but she was clearly upset with the prospect of her mother being upset with her and worse with the thought that she might be taken away from her mother. She said her mother never hit her or even raised her voice, but something was obviously wrong.

I called the mother and asked her to come to the school to talk about her daughter. She acted like any parent would when receiving such a call. She was terrified that something bad had happened. The school was within walking distance from her home, so it did not take long for the mother to walk to the school. I was waiting for her in the main office waiting room. She was a plain looking woman wearing a simple dress and worn shoes. Her hair was pulled back in a severe way. Her humble appearance was not a surprise, because it was a blue-collar neighborhood. I was, however, surprised at her age. She appeared to be in her late fifties. Maybe she was not that old; maybe life had worn her features down. I learned that she was 59 years old and was a former college instructor. She and her late husband lived a middle-class life for several years, but he became seriously ill and lingered in pain for almost eight years before passing away. His illness and care used up all of the family's financial resources. Their only daughter was adopted. They were excited about their adopted baby but two years after the adoption, her husband became gravely ill and could not work or help care for the little girl. The mother had to go to work, take time from work to care for her ailing husband, and somehow raise their daughter. When her husband passed away, she struggled financially and emotionally to survive and had to move from a middle-class neighborhood to a duplex in an economically depressed side of town. Daily life became a mighty struggle.

What the girl did not know and could not know is that her mother was slowly losing her grip on reality due to chronic grief and stress.

I told the mother that her daughter was concerned about her. When I asked the mother about the episode with the matches, she looked very puzzled. Until that point, she gave a very clear recap of her life and troubles and was very articulate and calm. She showed appropriate awareness of her surroundings, gave full answers to questions, and seemed very concerned about her daughter. But I could tell that the question about the matches troubled her. She did not know how to respond, it seemed. Her eyes drifted away as if she was trying to remember something that she could not capture. Finally, she said, *"It's very strange that you should ask about matches. I had a dream about matches. In the dream, I kept asking my daughter why there were so many spent matches on the floor in her room."* She did not remember what had happened, but she had a vague recollection of something about matches. She clearly needed help. She had lost her job because of her growing instability and essentially stayed in her duplex all day and had no interaction with anyone. They were barely surviving on government assistance.

We were able to make the appropriate referrals to service agencies that day while the student stayed with friends. It took several months, but the mother's mental condition was diagnosed; she was put on medication, and over time became functionally self-supporting. She found a job with DFCS and became a valuable member of the staff by working well with parents. Her daughter moved back in with her, and later graduated from high school and attended a local college.

On another referral, I was asked to speak to a ten-year-old elementary student who refused to go home with his mother one afternoon. The student was very small for his age, made straight A's, and was considered "odd" by his teachers and classmates.

When I got to the school, I saw a police car in front of the school and a police officer standing at the front door. The police officer asked me if I was there to see the little boy. When I confirmed I was, he said, "Thank, God!" and made a hasty retreat to his cruiser and left.

The principal met me at the door. I had not been to this school before so I did not know the principal. She was very calm but more grateful for my presence than she should have been. She quickly introduced herself and gave me a succinct summary of the situation.

She said the mother of the little boy told them to call the police because the little boy refused to go home with her or listen to any adult in the school, so they called the police. Of course, the police officer wanted nothing to do with this situation and I did not blame him for that.

I met the mother who was tall, thin, and so nervous that even her hair seemed to be filled with electricity. She said, *"I knew it would come to this. I've told my husband that it would come to this. Our child is out of control and he doesn't listen and he causes problems everywhere we go. I can't control him ...."* She went on until finally I turned to the principal and asked to see the little boy. The mother was still talking when I left the principal's office.

In the counselor's office sat a tiny little boy with big, black-rimmed glasses reading a book. I gave some type of benign greeting and he only looked up at me for a second before returning to his book. I asked him what he was reading. I did not see much point in introducing myself. With some kids, that formality in certain situations makes a bad situation worse, so I just started talking. I knew this was no ordinary ten-year-old when he held up the book. He was reading *The Silmarillion* by J.R.R. Tolkien and Christopher Tolkien. This was an unfinished book by the author of the *Lord of the Rings Trilogy* that was completed by his oldest son, Christopher. *The Silmarillion* is a very difficult book to read. How difficult? Consider this simplified description: *"The Silmarillion comprises five parts. The first part, Ainulindalë, tells of the creation of Eä, the "world that is". Valaquenta, the second part, gives a description of the Valar and Maiar, the supernatural powers in Eä. The next section, Quenta Silmarillion, which forms the bulk of the collection, chronicles the history of the events before and during the First Age. The fourth part, Akallabêth, relates the history of the Downfall of Númenor and its people, which takes place in the Second Age. The final part, Of the Rings of Power and the Third Age, is a brief account of the circumstances which led to and were presented in The Lord of the Rings (Wikipedia).*

I could not believe that this ten-year-old was actually reading this book, so as a true representative of the stupidity of all adults I asked a question that is really a statement of disbelief disguised as a question: "*Are you really reading that book?*" He looked up at me with large brown eyes magnified by his thick glasses and said, "*Why are you asking me stupid questions?*" This was a very good question for which I did not have a very good answer. So, I cut to the situation at hand. "*Why do you choose not to go home with your mother today?*" I asked. He replied, "*She's not really my mom, you know.*" I did not know where this was going, but I jumped in any way thinking that perhaps he was adopted. "*Who is she?*" I asked. "*She's an impersonator,*" he said nonchalantly. "*What do you mean?*" I asked with growing curiosity mixed with concern. "*Did you ever see the movie 'Invasion of the Body Snatchers.'?* I acknowledged that I had. He said with all seriousness, "*She came from a pod.*" Obviously, this kid is smarter than me; in fact, he's probably smarter than anyone in the building. Was he jerking my chain? Or was he delusional? While I was contemplating what to do next, he looked up from his book and said, "*You think I'm crazy, don't you?*" When in doubt, keep your mouth shut. I did. He was very uncomfortable with my silence. Finally, he said, "*Well, are you going to analyze me or something?*" I said, "*No, I just want you to go home with your mom.*" Then I added, "*Why don't we talk tomorrow when you come back to school.*" He said as he stood up, "*That's a good idea.*"

He left the counselor's office, walked past the main office, and went straight to his mother's car without a word to anyone. The mother, the principal, and the counselor watched him wordlessly and then turned to me and said in one voice, "*What happened?*" I simply said, "*I listened.*"

I met with the young boy several times during the school year. He was brilliant beyond measure. He was so intelligent his view of the world was unlike anyone else's, so he had a very difficult time relating to other people. He was in a gifted program, but the teacher was flummoxed about what to do for him because he was so smart. He mastered Algebra in the fourth grade and he was reading *Atlas Shrugged* in the fifth grade.

The little boy's father was a rising star in his company and was away from home a lot, and his mother was a housewife with a master's degree in literature.

The times I met with the little boy could not be called therapy or even counseling. In fact, they were not sessions either. I listened a lot while he talked about what he was reading or what he had heard on the news or read in the newspaper. The little boy's intelligence and level of insight was frightening to me; I cannot imagine how frightening it was to him. His critical thinking skills were on par with the brightest adult. How he gained such insight at his age without life experiences is still a puzzle to me.

Long before they became common, he was talking about small computers with powerful micro-processors that people would be able to carry around with them like a portable typewriter. He actually talked about a "wireless world" where people would not be limited by the location of the closest outlet. He talked about space travel by a specially equipped airplane that is propelled into space by a rocket. He said one day he had a new hobby. He was working on creating a language "*like Tolkien created the Elves language.*"

When I finally met his father, I was not totally surprised when he said that he could not relate to either his wife or his son. He said they far exceed his intellectual capacity. He told me that his son really enjoyed his sessions with me because he liked my sense of humor. The father said that was important for him to hear because he realized that there was very little humor in his house. He by nature had a good sense of humor but the intellectual weight of his son and wife seemed over time to have squeezed the humor out of him. He said he felt like he had to be more intellectual than humorous.

We talked about the advantages of being oneself, of living in a comfort zone, of releasing the pressure of being someone else. So, the father went back to being himself at home and he said his son greatly enjoyed the humor, the silliness that makes kids laugh. When he was out of town, he called his son and they started a ritual of exchanging silly jokes on the phone. I encouraged the little boy to share these jokes with his teachers and classmates because they viewed him solely as a "brain" and not as a kid.

My graduate training and work experiences did not help me work with the little boy. What helped me work with this student was a book I read during my sophomore year in college, a book by Herman Hesse. Hesse was a wonderfully gifted writer who won the Nobel Prize in Literature in 1946. For a period of time in the 1960s and 1970s, there was a rediscovery of his books, namely *Siddhartha, Steppenwolf,* and *The Glass Bead Game.* But my English professor said that one of Hesse's lesser-known books was one of his best, *Beneath the Wheel.* It was optional reading, but she encouraged us to read it. I did read it; it was superbly written and emotionally crushing.

Beneath the Wheel tells the story of Hans Giebenrath, a brilliant boy whose identity is solely that of an intellectual. He is never allowed to be a little boy, or a teenager, or a person. Much like the little boy I was working with, Hans had no existence, no personality, no likes or dislikes, no hobbies, and no friends. Everyone admired his intelligence but no one could relate to him, so no one got to know him or showed any concern or care for him. They simply admired his intelligence. The book describes Han's internal turmoil with his gift of intelligence and his unusual life in a small town and his unique view of the world.

However, his intelligence became a burden because he knew he was not like the other boys, no matter how much he wanted to be like them. His teachers pressured him constantly to live up to his intelligence, to live up to his potential, to do everything possible to get into the seminary, which in Germany at that time was the ultimate stamp of intellect and respect.

Hans worried about his intellect at that level but he soon found that he was as bright as most of the others, but most of the other boys had hobbies and friends. He formed one friendship with a classmate at the seminary in Maulbronn who in addition to being extraordinarily intelligent was also curious about life, so he pushed the rules and would sneak out and go into the local town to taste life. Han's friend was expelled but his influence on Hans remained profound because Hans sees that there is more to life than the academic world, but he is ill-prepared for the other aspects of life. As he questions his place in life, Hans' academic performance and his health suffer. His self-doubt and inner conflicts about life and his place in the world worsen. Which world would he embrace? Which world did he belong to? How could he learn social skills with no experience and no friends? How could he survive?

Finally, he is sent home in disgrace because he flunked out of seminary not because he lacked the intellectual prowess but because his study habits slacked off during a period of self-reflection and emotional turmoil and because the climate of the school was cold, sterile, and uncaring. None of the teachers showed any interest in the students other than as academic robots.

Back in his small town without friends, without social skills, and without his identity, he struggled to survive. His teachers and others did not see the suffering Hans; they saw Hans as the young man who wasted his God-given talent, so they shunned him. Hans was alone. He is often seen walking alone near the river. One day he is found drowned.

Hesse does not explicitly state that the death was suicide, because that is not the point. The point is that the education world and society did not let Hans become a full person. He was ground beneath the wheels of academics, high academic expectations, and paralyzing pressure with no regard for his socio-emotional development.

Hesse wrote *Beneath the Wheel* in 1906, but the message still resonates today—education and expectations are wonderful if they do not forget that kids are people, too, and kids must be allowed to enjoy and experience childhood. Kids need to learn about life; how to get along with others and how to settle arguments; how to laugh and play; how to explore possible hobbies, and how to fail and recover. Students whose only life is academics and whose only identity is academic excellence too often fail.

In my high school, two students come to mind that fit Hesse's description. One was awarded a full academic scholarship to a major university, but he could not handle the social part of college life. He dropped out after two years and he never went back to college. The other one also received a full academic scholarship to a major university and lasted one semester. In his situation, he found out that he was not the smartest student in college; he was smart, but so were many other students. He was not prepared for that, and he did not know how to interact socially as an equal. In high school, he did not have to work at social interaction, because that was not expected or required. After all, he was one of the brightest kids in school. That was all that was necessary; that was his identity.

I bought copies of *Beneath the Wheel* and gave them to the little boy's parents, the school counselor, and the teachers. I also gave a copy to the little boy. He was very interested in the book and he made a comment that I will never forget. *"I understand what Hans was going through and I feel lonely at times like he did. That's why I want to hear both you and my dad tell silly jokes and talk about life. That's what was missing in Hans' life and my life. He could not survive and if things didn't change in my life I'm not sure I would survive either."* Remember, this is a ten-year-old talking like this.

It took a while, but the role of his parents changed; they became more comfortable as parents. They seemed over time to be less intimidated by their son's intelligence and therefore they encouraged him to participate in activities such as Cub Scouts, a Chess Club at the local library, church activities, etc.

The family moved the next year after the father received a promotion at his Fortune 500 Company. I did not hear anything about the little boy or his family until almost ten years later when I received a package at work from Connecticut. Inside was a copy of *Beneath the Wheel* signed by the not-so-little boy with the following short note: "*I survived the Wheel.*"

I've worked hard over the years to understand what motivates people, what drives people, and what factors bring the changes necessary to create conditions for children that will make their lives better and their futures more promising. That sounds so naïve but I cannot think of anything more important.

Throughout the history of mankind and in the historical records and opinions and discoveries of mankind, there has always been and there will continue to be a focus on living conditions – the quality of life. Anthropologists reconstruct civilizations to learn about the circumstances of life during the height of various civilizations. They study the social, cultural, and physical climate of civilizations while we often compare the conditions of life in the United States with other parts of the world. And closer to home, we compare our neighborhoods with other neighborhoods on elements such as safety, traffic, access to food and services, access to medical care, access to entertainment and shopping, the quality of the infrastructure, the reputation of the schools and much more.

We are always looking for ways to improve the condition of our lives. That's personal and community climate – the conditions for life. Many of our schools have floundered because we have not focused on the right things; namely, we have not been attuned to the climate of schools – the conditions for learning and living. The climate in some schools is horrible and children suffer because of it. Adults in those schools show no regard for students' feelings or needs nor the conditions for teachers. Yet, I've seen schools that are safe and nurturing havens for students

- where students cannot wait to get to school and would stay all night if they could. Schools where students are engaged in the school, where teachers and other school staff members show in various ways how much they care about the students and where the camaraderie among teachers is a solid bond of support and encouragement. These are schools where culture and care permeate the school so deeply that it feels like a warm home. The students and teachers laugh, learn, and cry together. In these schools no one misses the hurt on the face of students or staff members – no one is ignored or forgotten. These positive climates exist even in schools where the communities are mired in poverty.

It is a moral imperative and responsibility to create conditions at home, in the communities, and at school that build a network of support for all children. The importance of school climate as part of the overly world of children cannot be ignored or understated any longer.

As my journey with children and characters slows while I approach the next bend in the road, I only have one wish and that is to be remembered as someone who was dedicated to and was a messenger for improving the conditions in schools for all children to learn, thrive, live, and grow.

REFERENCES

Alliance for Excellent Education press release, (September 12, 2013).

Arcia, Emily, "Achievement and Enrollment Status on Suspended Students," *Education and Urban Society*, Volume 38 (3) (2006): 359-369, doi:10.1177/0013 124506286947.

Bao, Zhenzhou, Dongping Li, Wei Zhang, Yanhui Wang, "School Climate and Delinquency among Chinese Adolescents: Analyses of Effortful Control as a Moderator and Deviant Peer Group Affiliation as a Mediator," *Journal of Abnormal Child Psychology*, 43 (2015): 81-93. doi:10.1007/s10802-014-9903-8.

Bosworth, K., L. Ford, and Diley Hernandez, "School Climate Factors Contributing to Student and Faculty Perceptions of Safety in Select Arizona Schools," *Journal of School Health*, Volume 81 (4) (2011): 194-201. doi:10.1111/j.1746-1561.2010.00579.x.

Brand, S. R.D. Felner, A. Seitsinger, A. Burns, and N. Bolton, "A large scale study of the assessment of the social environment of middle and secondary schools: the validity and utility of teachers' ratings of school climate, cultural pluralism, and safety problems for understanding school effects and school improvement," *Journal of School Psychology,* Volume 46 (5) (October 2008): 507-535.

Cash, Anne, Katrina Debnam, Tracy Waasdorp, Mary Wahl, Catherine P. Bradshaw, "Adult and student interactions in nonclassroom settings," *Journal of Educational Psychology*, (April 2018), http://psycnet.apa.org/2018-14328-001.

Cerezo, Fuensanta and Manuel Ato, "Social Status, Gender, Classroom Climate and Bullying among Adolescents Pupils," *Annals of Psychology*, Volume 26 (1) (2010): 137-144, http://www.siis.net/documentos/ficha/183784.pdf.

Chiaki, Konishi, Yasuo Miyazaki, and Shelly Hymel, "Investigating associations between school climate and bullying in secondary schools: Multilevel contextual effects modeling," *School Psychology International*, Volume 38 (3) (February 2017): 240-263.

Cohen, Jonathan, "School Climate Policy and Practice Trends: A Paradox," *Teachers College Record*, February 28, 2014 – Retrieved from The National School Climate Center – School Policy 2017.

Connell, Nadine, Nina Barbieri, and Jennifer M. Reingle Gonzalez, "Understanding School Effects on Students' Willingness to Report Peer Weapon Carrying," *Youth Violence and Juvenile Justice*, Volume 13 (3) (2015): 258-289. doi:10.1177/1541204014544512.

Costenbader, Virginia and Samia Markson, "School Suspension: A Study with Secondary School Students" *Journal of School Psychology*, Volume 36 (1) (1998): 59-82, doi:10.1016/S0022-4405(97)00050-2; Phi Delta Kappa International, *The 2013 PDK/Gallup Poll on Public Schools* (Bloomington: Delta Kappa International, 2013).

Debnam, Katrina, Sarah L. Johnson, and Catherine P. Bradshaw, "Examining the Association between Bullying and Adolescent Concerns about Teen Dating Violence," *Journal of School Health,* Volume 84 (7) (2014): 421-428. doi:10.1111 /josh.12170.

DeBono, Edward, "Lateral Thinking," Harper and Row, (1967).

Doumas, Diana, Aida Midgett, and April D. Johnston, "Substance Use and Bullying Victimization Among Middle and High School Students: Is Positive School Climate a Protective Factor?" *Journal of Addiction and Offending Counseling*, Volume 38 (1) (April 2017): 2-14.

Ertesvag, Sigrun and Erling Roland, "Professional Cultures and Rates of Bullying," *School Effectiveness and School Improvement*, Volume 26, (2) (2014): 195-214. doi:10.10 80/09243453.2014.944547.

Espelage, Dorothy Joshua R. Polanin, and Sabina K. Low, "Teacher and Staff Perceptions of School Environment as Predictors of Student Aggression, Victimization, and Willingness to Intervene in Bullying Situations," *School Psychology Quarterly*, Volume 29 (3) (2014): 287-305. doi:10.1037/spq0000072.

Espelage, Dorothy, Joshua R. Polanin, and Sabina K. Low, "Teacher and Staff Perceptions of School Environment as Predictors of Student Aggression, Victimization, and Willingness to Intervene in Bullying Situations," *School*

Psychology Quarterly, Volume 29 (3) (2014): 287-305. doi:10.1037/spq0000072

Ferrans, Silvia and Robert L. Selman, "How Students' Perceptions of the School Climate Influence Their Choice to Upstand, Bystand, or Join Perpetrators of Bullying," *Harvard Educational Review*, Volume 84 (2) (2014):162-187. doi:10.17763/haer.84.2. h4883134101651mm.

Ford, C., Parker, J. Salim, R. Goodman, S. Logan, W. Henley, "The relationship between exclusion from school and mental health: a secondary analysis of the British Child and Adolescent Mental Health Surveys 2004 and 2007," *Psychological Medicine*, (2017) 1 doi: 10.1017/S003329171700215X

Gallo, Ciara, "School Climate, Hope, and Readiness to Change: A Mediation Model" (2018). *University Research Symposium*. 58. https://ir.library.illinoisstate. edu/rsp_urs/58.

Gendron, Brian, Kirk R. Williams, and Nancy G. Guerra, "An Analysis of Bullying among Students within Schools: Estimating the Effects of Individual Normative Beliefs, Self-Esteem, and School Climate," *Journal of School Violence*, Volume 10 (2) (2011): 150-164. doi:10.1080/15388220. .539166.

Giovazolias, Theodoros, Elias Kourkoutas, Effrosyni Mitsopoulou, and Maria Georgiadi, "The Relationship between Perceived School Climate and the Prevalence of Bullying Behavior in Greek Schools: Implications for

Preventive Inclusive Strategies" *Procedia Social and Behavioral Sciences*, Volume 5 (2010): 2208-2215. doi:10.1016/j. sbspro. 2010.07.437.

Glaser, Barney and Anselm Strauss, *The Discovery of Grounded Theory: Strategies for Qualitative Research* (New York, Aldine de Gruyter Publishers, 1967).

Goldstein, Sara, Amy Young, and Carol Boyd, "Relational Aggression at School: Associations with School Safety and Social Climate," *Journal of Youth Adolescence*, Volume 37 (2008): 641-654. doi:10.1007/s10964-007-9192-4.

Gottfredson, D.C., D. B. Wilson, and S. S. Najaka. 2002. "School-based Crime Prevention." In *Evidence-Based Crime Prevention*, edited by L. W. Sherman, D. P. Farrington, B.C. Welsh, and D. L. MacKenzie. (London: Routledge, 2002).

Gregory, Anne, Dewey Cornell, Xitao Fan, Peter Sheras, Tse-Hua Shih, and Francis Huang, "Authoritative School Discipline: High School Practices Associated with Lower Bullying and Victimization," *Journal of Educational Psychology*, Volume 102 (2) (2010): 483-496.

Han, Ziqiang, Guirong Zhang, and Haibo Zhang, "School Bullying in Urban China: Prevalence and Correlation with School Climate," *International Journal of Environmental Research and Public Health,* (2017), 14(10), 1116, doi: 10.3390/ijerph14101116.

Hemphill, Sheryl, John W. Toumbourou, Todd I. Herrenkohl, Barbara J. McMorris, and Richard F. Catalano, "The Effect of School Suspensions and Arrests on Subsequent Adolescent Antisocial Behavior in Australia and the United States," *Journal of Adolescent Health*, Volume 39 (5) (2006): 736-744, doi:10.1016/j.jado health.2006.05.010/

Hemphill, Sheryl, Todd I. Herrenkohl, Stephanie M. Plenty, John W. Toumbourou, Richard F. Catalano, and Barbara J. McMorris, "Pathways from School Suspension to Adolescent Nonviolent Antisocial Behavior in Students in Victoria, Australia and Washington State, United States," *Journal of Community Psychology*, Volume 40 (3) (2012): 301-318, http://www. ncbi.nlm.nih.gov/pmc/articles /PMC 3774047/.

Huang, Frances, and Dewey Cornell, "The Relationship of School Climate and Out-of-School Suspensions," *Children and Youth Services Review*, (August 2018), doi: 10.1016/j.childyouth.2018.08.013.

Jeong, Seokjin, Jaya Davis, and Youngsun Han, "Who Becomes More Violent among Korean Adolescents? Consequences of Victimization in School," *Criminal Behavior and Mental Health*, Volume 25 (2) (2014): 141-155. doi:10.1002 /cbm.1919.

Klein, Jennifer, Dewey Cornell, and Timothy Konold, "Relationships between Bullying School Climate and Student Risk Behaviors," *School Psychology Quarterly*,

Volume 27 (3) (September 2012): 154-169, doi: 10.1037/a0029350.

LeBlanc, Line, Raymond Swisher, Frank Vitaro, and Richard E. Tremblay, "High School Social Climate and Antisocial Behavior: A 10-Year Longitudinal and Multilevel Study," *Journal of Research on Adolescence*, Volume 18 (3 (2008): 395-419. doi:10.1111/j.1532-7795.2008.00565.x.

Lenzi, Michela, Alessio Vieno, Gianluca Gini, Tiziana Pozzoli, Massimiliano Pastore, Massimo Santinello, and Frank J. Elgar, "Perceived Teacher Unfairness, Instrumental Goals, and Bullying Behavior in Early Adolescence," *Journal of Interpersonal Violence*, Volume 29 (10) (2013): 1834-1849. doi:10.1177/08862 60513511694.

Lhamon, Catherine, *Dear Colleague Letter*, United States Departments of Education Office of Civil Rights, 2014, http://www2.ed.gov/about/offices/list/ocr/letters/colleague -resourcecomp-201410.pdf.

Liu, John, *"The Suspension Spike: Changing the Discipline Culture in NYC's Middle Schools,"* (New York: New York City Government Report, July 2013), https://comptroller. nyc.gov/wp-content/uploads/2013/07/NYC_Middle Schools_Summary.pdf.

Lori M. Phillips, Lori, "Influence of Student Discipline Referrals on School Climate in a K-12 Urban Public School District," Dissertation (June 2018), Walden University.

Low, Sabrina and Mark Van Ryzin, "The Moderating Effects of School Climate on Bullying Prevention Efforts," *School Psychology Quarterly*, Volume 29 (3) (2014): 306-319. doi:10.1037/spq0000073.

Ma, X., "Sense of Belonging to School: Can Schools Make a Difference?" *The Journal of Educational Research*, Volume 96 (6) (2003): 340-349.

Marks, Helen, "Student Engagement in Instructional Activity," *American Educational Research*, Volume 37 (1) (Spring 2016): 153-184.

McGiboney Garry and Dennis Kramer, "The Relationship between School Climate and Student Achievement," Paper presented at the Youth Issues Summit, Callaway Gardens, Georgia (March 9, 2012).

Megan Eliot, Dewey Cornell, Anne Gregory, and Xitao Fan, "Supportive School Climate and Student Willingness to Seek Help for Bullying and Threats of Violence," *Journal of School Psychology*, Volume 48 (6) (2010): 533-553.

Mehta, S.B., D. Cornell, X. Fan, and A. Gregory, "Bullying Climate and School Engagement in Ninth-Grade Students," *The Journal of School Health*, Volume 83, 2013, http://dx.doi.org/10.1111/j .1746-1561.2012.00746.

Mitchell, Roxanne, Lisa Kensler, and Megan Tschannen-Moran, "Student Trust in Teachers and Student Perceptions of Safety: Positive Predictors of School Identification with School," *International Journal of*

Leadership in Education: Theory and Practice, (May 10, 2016): www.tandfonline.com /doi/abs/10.1080/ 136031 24.2016.115721.

Morris, Edward, and Brea L. Perry, "The Punishment Gap: School Suspension and Racial Disparities in Achievement," *Society for the Study of Social Problems*, Volume 63 (1) (February 2016): 68 86,https://doi.org/10.1093/socpro /spv026.

National Center for Educational Statistics, *Public School Safety, and Discipline: 2013-2014. Institute of Education Sciences* (Washington, D.C.: United States Department of Education, 2013).

Pecjak, Sonja and Tina Pirc, "Bullying and Perceived School Climate: Victims' and Bullies' Perspective," *Studia Psychologica*, Volume 59 (1) (2017): 22-33.

Raskauskas Juliana, Janet Gregory, Shane T. Harvey Fathimath Rifshana, Palmerston North, and Ian M. Evans, "Bullying among Primary School Children in New Zealand: Relationships with Prosocial Behaviour and Classroom Climate," *Journal of Educational Research* (2009), 1-13.

Reaves, Samantha Susan McMahon, Sophia Duffy, and Linda Ruitz, "The Test of Time: A Meta-Analysis Review of the Relation between School Climate and Problem Behavior," *Aggression and Violent Behavior*, (March 2018), Volume 39, pp. 100-108.

Robert J. Reid, N. Andrew Peterson, Joseph Hughey, and Pauline Garcia-Reid, "School Climate and Adolescent Drug

Use: Mediating Effects of Violence Victimization in the Urban High School Context," *The Journal of Primary Prevention*, Volume 27 (2006): 281-292. doi:10.1007/s10935-006-0035-y.

Silver, Nate, "The Signal and the Noise," Allan Lane Publishers, (2012).

Simmons-Morton, Bruce, Aria Davis Crump, Denise L. Haynie, and Keith E. Saylo, "Student-School Bonding and Adolescent Problem Behavior," *Health Education Research*, Volume 13 (1) (1999): 99-107. doi:10.1093/her/14.1.99.

Stader, David, Thomas J. Graca, and David W. Stevens, "Teachers and the Law: Evolving Legal Issues," *The Clearing House: A Journal of Educational Strategies, Issues, and Ideas*, Volume 83 (3) (2010): 73-75. doi:10.1080/00098651003662148.

Steinberg, Matthew, Elaine Allensworth, and David W. Johnson, "Student and Teacher Safety in Chicago Public Schools: The Roles of Community Context and School Social Organization," (Consortium on Chicago School Research at the University of Chicago Urban Education Institute 2011).

Storer, Heather, Erin A. Casey, and Todd I. Herrenkohl. "Developing 'Whole School' Bystander Interventions," *Children and Youth Services Review*, Volume 74, (March 2017): 87-95.

Syversten, Amy, Constance A. Flannagan, and Michael D. Stout, "Code of Silence: Students' Perceptions of School

Climate and Willingness to Intervene in a Peer's Dangerous Plan," *Journal of Educational Psychology*, Volume 101 (1) (2009): 219-232, http://dx.doi.org/10.1037/a0013246.

Tracy Evian Wassdorp, Elise T. Pas, Benjamin Zablotxky, and Catherine Bradshaw, "Ten-Year Trends in Bullying and Related Attitudes Among 4th-12th Graders," *Pediatrics, American Academy of Pediatrics,* (May 2017 online), doi: 10.1542/ peds.2016-2615, PubMed 28562260.

Turner, Isobel, Katherine J. Reynolds, Eunro Lee, Emina Subasic, and David Bromhead, "Well-Being, School Climate, and the Social Identity Process: A Latent Growth Model Study of Bullying Perpetration and Peer Victimization," *School Psychology Quarterly*, Volume 29 (3) (2014): 320-325. doi:10.1037/spq0000074.

U.S. Secret Service and U.S. Department of Education, "Threat Assessment in Schools: A Guide to Managing Threatening Situations and to Creating Safe School Climates" (Washington, D.C.: U.S. Department of Education, 2004), https://www 2.ed.gov/admins/lead/ safety/threatassessmentguide.pdf.

Veiga Simão, A.M., P. Costa Ferreira, I. Freire, A.P. Caetano, M.J. Martins, and C. Vieira, "Adolescent Cyber victimization – Who they turn to and their perceived school climate," *Journal of Adolescence*, Volume 58, (2017): 12-23, doi: 10.1016/j.adolescence.2017.04.009.

Wang Mong-Te and Thomas J. Dishion, "The Trajectories of Adolescents' Perceptions of School Climate, Deviant Peer

Affiliation, and Behavioral Problems during the Middle School Years," *Journal of Research on Adolescence*, Volume 22, (1) (2012): 40-53. doi:10.1111/j.1532-7795.2011.00763.x.

Wang, Zhen, ChengYu, Wei Zhang, Yuanyuan Chen, Jianjun Zhu, and Qiaoy Liu, "School Climate and Adolescent Aggression: A Moderated Mediation Model Involving Deviant Peer Affiliation and Sensation Seeking," *Journal of Personality and Individual Differences*, (December 2017), Volume 119 (1), pp. 301-306.

Welsh, Wayne, "The Effects of School Climate on School Disorder," *The Annals of the American Academy of Political and Social Science*, Volume 567 (1) (January 1, 2000): 88-107.

Welsh, Wayne, "The Effects of School Climate on School Disorder," *The Annals of the American Academy of Political and Social Science*, 567, no. 1 (2000): 88-107. doi:10.1177/000271620056700107.

Welsh, Wayne, "The Effects of School Climate on School Disorder," *The Annals of the American Academy of Political and Social Science*, Volume 567 (1) (2000): 88-107. doi:10.1177/000271620056700107.

Welsh, Wayne, Jack R. Greene, and Patricia H. Jenkins, "School Disorder: The Influence of Individual, Institutional, and Community Factors," *Criminology*, Volume 37 (1) (1999): 73-116. doi:10.1111/j.1745-9125.1999.tb00480.x.

Welsh, Wayne, Patricia H. Jenkins, Jack R. Greene, Dawn Caron, Eric Hoffman, Ellen Kurtz, Donna Perone, and Robert Stokes, *Building a Culture and Climate of Safety in Public Schools in Philadelphia: School-based Management and Violence Reduction, Paper for the National Institute of Justice* (Washington, D.C.: United States Department of Justice, National Institute of Justice, 1996), https://www.ncjrs.gov/pdffiles1/Photocopy/171631NCJRS.pdf.

Zaykowski, Heather and Whitney Gunter, "Youth Victimization: School Climate or Deviant Lifestyles?" *Journal of Interpersonal Violence*, Volume 27 (3) (2012): 431-452. doi:10.1177/0886260511421678.

Author

Garry McGiboney has a Ph.D. in both school psychology and administration. He is a member of several professional organizations and has served on state and national boards. Dr. McGiboney was appointed by the Governor of Georgia to serve on the Joint Study Committee on Mental Health Access, the Joint Study Committee on the Establishment of a State Leadership Academy, and the Senate Study Committee on Dyslexia. He also serves by appointment on the Georgia Supreme Court's Justice for Children Committee; the Juvenile Detention Alternative Initiative Steering Committee of the Georgia Council on Criminal Justice Reform; and the Georgia Accrediting Commission. He has over 30 professional journal publications on psychology and youth-related issues, and he is the author of several books. Dr. McGiboney has been interviewed by *CNN, NBC, CBS, ABC*, and many regional and local television and radio affiliates. Also, he was featured in a bullying awareness program on the *Nickelodeon Network* and on an *A&E* television special on school violence. Additionally, Dr. McGiboney appeared in a U.S. Department of Education video production of *Emergency Preparedness for Families*. He has been quoted in *Time* Magazine, *USA Today, Los Angeles Times, Wall Street Journal,* and other publications, including the international press, on many topics. He is the recipient of several awards, including NAACP Educator of the Year; the National Association of School Psychologists National Friend of Children Award; Georgia School Counselors Advocate of the Year Award; two time recipient of the Georgia Association of School Nurses Hero Award; School Social Workers Association of Georgia Friend of Children Award; Mental Health America Board Member of the Year, United States EPA Children's Health Hero Award, Georgia Appleseed Law Center Good Apple Award, and others. Recently, he was inducted into the Georgia Board of Regents Hall of Fame for his career-long efforts on behalf of children.